STRANGERS I HAVE KNOWN

MELISSA KOTLER SCHWARTZ

Published in the United States of America by
Melissa Kotler Schwartz, 2016

Photos by Tina Gutierrez Arts-Photography

Cover illustration by Jane Sayre Denny

ISBN: 978-0-9863372-0-8

for Steve, Olivia and Sam

AUTHOR'S NOTE

The people in this book are real strangers to me. I have refrained, with a few exceptions, from sharing details that would reveal their identity. Most of the time, I didn't know their names. I hope you enjoy the moments I shared with them as much as I did.

Contents

Introduction

I. Strangers Around Town

A Yellow Paper That Says Thank You to a Stranger 2
Twice-a-Day Friends 3
The Oil Man 5
Company on a Bench 7
Fire-Breathing Dragon 10
Complete Complimentary Strangers 11
The Man with the Novel Voice 14
An Un-Unencounter 16

II. Strangers in the News

Meet-Up in the Ball Pit 20
An Encounter with a Stranger Can Glisten Like Pearls 21
Stranger in the Attic 24
The Hermit of North Pond, Maine 26
For the Love of People 28
The Heartwarming Story of a Fuzzy Bear's Travels 30
What I Learned from a "Writer of Dark Fiction" 32

III. Strangers You Learn Something From

Mrs. Pepper, Dangling Lemons and
Directionally Challenged Rolls 36
Betting on Strangers 40
The Parrot Lover from Brazil 41
Flasher 43
Thirty Minutes in the Life of a Volunteer Reading Tutor 45
"I Never Buy Retail" 49
Happy to Help? 52
Crossing Paths in Johnny Appleseed Country 54

IV. Strangers Helping Strangers

Sidewalk Hero 58
"I'm No Angel" 60

Almost Heaven, One Tire at a Time 61
Starbucks Grande 63
I Don't Know You, But Thanks for Opening the Door 65
Hannah Brencher—The Love Letter Writer 66
A Story of True Courage 67
The Smiling Elephant, Part 1 69

V. Mystical Strangers

The Smiling Elephant, Part 2 72
Broken Blue 74
Down on Your Luck, Wish for a Red Fox 76
Transported in Time 77
It's Nothing but an Evil Eye 78
Guardian Angel 80
The Waving Man 82
The Lucky Cookie 86

VI. Young Strangers

A Perfect Circle 88
Post Office: Roselawn, Ohio, A Sunny August
Afternoon after Lunch 90
A Splendid Summer Day 92
Stranger in the Cabin 94
The Girl on the Rock 97
For the Love of French Fries 100

VII. Strangers on the Job

The Phlebotomist and Me 104
Paid to Play with Dogs 106
Remember the Clerk Rules the Roost 108
The Manicurist Who Never Did Her Homework 111
Strangers with Word Limits 113
The Sunnyside Up Waitress 115
The Most Charming Pizza Delivery Man on Earth 118

VIII. Strangers in Close Quarters

Here's Where You Get Off 122
The Thoughts of a Stranger Running Out of Time 126
Mr. Flirt 128

The Empty Seat Next to You 131
Her Kitchen Story 133
Soldier on Board 136
Friends in a Jiffy 139

IX. Strangers with Chutzpah

Never Meddle with a Locksmith 142
One More Way to Use a Cultivator 144
Near Naked Yoga 146
The iPad Snooper 148
Of Course You Will 150
Pumping a Captive Audience 152

X. Strangers in Different Circles

Thirty Thousand Strangers under the Age of Thirty 156
Hey, What's That Monkey Doing on My Head? 159
Mission: Talk to Strangers 161
Breakfast with a Psychic Seeker 163
Dasher, Dancer, Prancer and All Things Christmas 167
Strangers on a Campus 169
Pitter Patter All Night Long 172
A World of Its Own 174
Strangers Using Strange Words 177
Medicine for What Ails You 178

XI. Like-Minded Strangers

The Artist in the Paint Department 182
Southern Sisterhood 184
A Sweet Connection 185
Revisiting the Roselawn Post Office 188
Delivery Shot 190
Tea with Strangers 191
Rush-Hour Rainbow 192

Resources 193

Acknowledgements 197

About the Author 201

INTRODUCTION

Why do I talk to strangers? After all, I'll never truly know them, or, in most cases, even see them again. My answer is clear—my life is made all the better from these momentary connections, and I know that the same is true for these passersby. It's better to have known each other briefly than to not have known each other at all.

People often worry about talking to strangers, but the vast majority of people are safe to talk to. And if they're not, we can probably tell right away. UC Berkeley psychologist Dacher Keltner, working with a team of other researchers, discovered that it takes most people only "20 seconds to detect whether a stranger is genetically inclined to be trustworthy, kind or compassionate."

I'm convinced that friendly interactions, even those that last only a few seconds, make the world a better place. I'm not the only one. Research has shown the value of connecting with the people we encounter in our daily lives—it can bring you health benefits as well as brighten your day. Nicholas Epley, John Templeton Keller Professor of Behavioral Science at the University of Chicago Booth School of Business, and Julianna Schroeder, PhD '14, have discovered that talking with strangers, even if we don't share anything in common, raises our level of happiness. But you don't need the research to know it. You can feel it when a conversation with a stranger comes to an end and you both wave goodbye. Perhaps you've shared a laugh, a moment of bonding, a sliver of truth or a bit of wisdom.

Why do I write about strangers? I write about them in order to document their stories, which are so intriguing to me. And because I want other people to read them and know the strangers I have known.

Take a moment to consider all the good in your life that has come from meeting strangers. If we think about it, many great conversations and much good luck has come to us because we were willing to take the risk and talk to a person we didn't know. Many people believe that some people are lucky and some are not, when the truth—according to sociologist and happiness expert Christine Carter, Ph.D. of UC Berkeley's Greater Good Science Center—is that we often create our own luck through social interaction with people we don't know.

This book is a collection of my favorite encounters with strangers I have known. I've found fascinating people in random locations, from my podiatrist's waiting room to a West Virginia auto repair shop to a hometown dog show. It's been quite a journey. I couldn't have imagined that writing about a woman who pointed out parrots to me on telephone wires in Sarasota, Florida, would connect me to people in Brazil who thanked me for writing about her. It's the endless mystery and surprise that keeps me talking with strangers on a daily basis.

So I hope this book inspires you to strike up conversations while waiting for a cup of coffee, taking in a ball game or picking up a few things at the store. It's small gestures like these that can make the world a better place, and will likely bring you greater luck, health and happiness. Who wouldn't want that in their lives?

Good luck, and all the best to you,

Melissa

STRANGERS AROUND TOWN

A Yellow Paper That Says Thank You to a Stranger

"I'm looking for the kind White Haired Lady who stopped to give me assistance … I want to Thank You."

This message on a yellow piece of paper posted on the bulletin board of the IGA grocery store in Reading, Ohio, was the coolest thing I had seen all day—someone taking the time to thank a stranger who had helped her after an accident.

I realize that this person might search and search and never find the lady who had helped her, but the fact that she had reached out and tried was heartwarming. Does the old-fashioned bulletin board still bring people together? I wondered.

Yes, I decided. A message like this, even if it never reaches the "kind Lady" it's meant for, reminds everyone who reads it to feel grateful for strangers who help others out.

Twice-a-Day Friends

Did you ever wonder about the regulars at restaurants? The ones who walk in the door and the waitresses already have their drinks, the ones so predictable it's like the wind never changes course. Even more amazing are the regulars who eat at the same restaurant twice a day.

Today I started up a conversation with one of those regulars, though I hadn't realized that yet. He sat kitty corner to me at the counter at Frisch's restaurant on Red Bank Road. The man had round tortoise-shell glasses that were a bit too large, thinning, reddish hair, and a white dress shirt and tan pants. I guessed he was in his early seventies. I didn't know if he wanted to talk to me or not, but I decided all I can do is try. I said hello, and then I took a bite of my eggs. "Oh, they're cold," I said.

"Send them back," he said.

"That's my plan, if I can catch her." I fumbled with my napkin.

"Mary," he called out to the waitress picking up an order. "Her eggs are cold."

Mary came right over. "Sorry," she said. "I'll get this taken care of for you."

I smiled at her and turned to the man who had just helped me.

"Thank you," I said.

He gave me a sideways smile. It pays to know the regulars, I thought.

"So do you have a busy day or a not-too-busy day?" I asked him. I didn't want to assume that he was retired.

"Busy," the man who sat next to him said. "But he'll be back at 12 for lunch." This man wore a navy blue workman's uniform with his name embroidered in gold on the pocket—*Jim*.

I thought it was funny how Jim had answered for his friend, and then he said, "We always have breakfast and lunch together."

Their routines might seem boring or predictable to the person who is always trying new restaurants, but it was clear to me that they took comfort in meeting up at the counter, in being twice-a-day friends. There are days we all need to believe that the wind never changes course.

The Oil Man

Most of us have strangers in our lives, people we often see on the street, in the library or the grocery store, but never talk to. We may make up stories about their lives in order to try to understand them. We might even create names for them. I call one of my strangers The Oil Man.

I began seeing him a few years ago on a route I often drive. The first thing I noticed was that he began his day oily. He wore an auto mechanic's uniform, but it was never clean. His hair was greasy and swept way over to the side.

He appeared to be well into his sixties, very worn, like one of those leather-skinned guys in the old Western movies. I realized he could be much younger, and not have aged well. Sometimes, I just wanted to clean him up. Every time I saw him I thought, he has no one to take care of him.

Once, I happened to park my car next to an auto shop. I was surprised, when I glanced inside the old garage, to see The Oil Man working on a car. I could tell he enjoyed his work because he was completely focused on some part of the engine of an old red Jeep. He never looked up.

A year passed and the auto shop went out of business. I didn't see The Oil Man for a long time and I wondered how he was doing. I hoped that he got another job.

Then on a wintry weekday afternoon, as the snow was coming down heavily, I spotted him. Things had clearly gotten worse. He was walking with great difficulty on crutches and as I got closer I noticed that he was missing part of his right leg. I gasped. It was freezing out. A couple of teenagers passed him on the street, but he paid no attention to them.

I wondered if he had been in an accident. He looked gaunt and tired. Why did he have to go out in the snow? Where was he going?

After that, I started seeing him almost every day, limping down the streets—any time of day, any kind of weather. Sometimes, I saw him heading north, sometimes south. He never talked to anyone, he just kept moving.

I said a prayer whenever I saw him, hoping that he would be okay.

One day, we passed each other on the sidewalk. I smiled at him. He looked right through me.

Company on a Bench

I don't think I would have ever met the two men who sat next to one another on a nearby park bench if my puppy, Louie, hadn't been with me. Puppies are people magnets and when the two men passing the time smiled at him, I brought Louie closer to say hi.

"What kind of dog is he?" the man with the dark blond hair and captivating blue eyes asked. His face was very tan and perfectly wrinkled. His eyes were so compelling that I wanted to ask him where he got them, as if I could purchase them in a store. He looked like a sea captain to me, one from a children's book.

"A Havanese," I said.

"I haven't seen one of those before."

"These dogs were originally bred in Spain," I said. "Sailors took them on ships from Spain to Cuba. They would trade them for goods."

The sea captain looked at Louie again. He reached out his hand and Louie sniffed it. Then he petted the side of his neck.

The other man followed his lead, reaching out cautiously to pet Louie's head. He was the opposite of the sea captain, pale, with eyes that looked worn and sad. A few wisps of hair crisscrossed the top of his balding head. On this hot September day, with the sun baking on their backs, the balding man wore a black trench coat with a belt tightly wrapped around his waist. "I've been sitting here a few hours with my friend," he said proudly. I wasn't sure if he knew his friend's name, but it was clear that being with the sea captain meant something to him that he wanted to share with me.

The sea captain looked at Louie. "I work at an animal shelter as a volunteer from 12:00 at night to 5:00 in the morning," he said. "We have cats bigger than your dog."

"What do you do at the shelter?" I asked.

"Oh, I just help out. I feed them and hold them and do what needs to be done."

The trench coat man pointed a pale, swollen finger at Louie. "He's not interested in us, too much going on at the park." He looked disappointed, as if Louie were letting him down.

I turned and looked back at the soccer game that was happening behind us. A coach was yelling at some boys to get the ball. Louie stood still, watching and listening to the sounds of the coach and the crowd cheering. All three of us watched silently as I tried to find words to alleviate the unhappiness I felt emanating from this man. I wanted to say something kind, but I just couldn't think of anything. And I had to be somewhere.

I settled for "Now, say goodbye, Louie." I added a smile. "It's been nice talking with you both."

"Take care, Louie," the sea captain said.

The gloomy-eyed man didn't say anything. I wished he had a pet, a dog like Louie who could be his friend. Maybe he did, but I didn't think so. He could tell his furry friend so many things that he may not be able to share with his companion on the bench.

Fire-Breathing Dragon

I'm in a short line at the bagel shop waiting for my pumpernickel bagel to toast. Behind me, a man in his golden years is breathing down my neck like a two-year-old, hoping to get his bagel before I get mine, even though I'm ahead of him.

He wants it now. We live in a hurry-up society and this neck-breathing can be one of the unwanted byproducts. Here he is, past his prime and yet he has learned nothing about patience.

I hear a thud and see my bagel drop out of a large industrial toaster. "What would you like on it?" the curly-haired young man behind the counter asks.

"I'll have a little cream cheese with tomatoes." I paused and then added, "And some capers, too." Something about the capers just about took the fire-breathing dragon over the edge—he got even closer to me and tapped his foot.

I pulled my charge card out of my wallet to pay. Then it was finally his turn.

"How are you today, sir?" the cashier asked him.

"I'm having a terrific day," he said.

Right, I said to myself. I can tell you're taking in all that the day has to offer. Now that you've got your bagel, how long will it be before you breathe your fire down someone else's neck?

Complete Complimentary Strangers

I can live for two months on a good compliment.
~ Mark Twain

This week three complete strangers complimented me.
And yes, I'm writing about it, because compliments
from complete strangers are a big deal. You're getting a
compliment because something you did charmed them.
Yes, charmed them.

(Hmm. Why do we say "complete strangers"? If someone's
a stranger, then he's always a complete one, right? I
mean, no one ever refers to someone as an "incomplete
stranger.") Anyway, don't tell me that a compliment from
a stranger doesn't do anything for you. It should do more
for you than one from someone you know, because it
means that you've made an immediate impression.

I'm still basking in my compliments, and here they are:

Compliment Number 1

There I was at Waffle House, finishing my pecan waffle,
just enjoying gazing at the various people at the counter.
The busboy, who was really a busman, came up to clear
my plate and as he approached he looked right at my face
and said, "You're beautiful."

I could have melted right there, like the chocolate chips
in my waffle. He looked at me again and said, "Really
beautiful."

That's it. I loved hearing that. I loved him. I don't care if
he says that to every woman at Waffle House. As long as I

don't see him dishing it out to other women, I'm happy.

"Thank you," I said and went up to pay my bill.

Compliment Number 2

When I got out of my car at the Goodwill drop-off center, I noticed an attractive man in his forties coming down the sidewalk to help me. His blond hair was so straight—kid straight, not adult straight. How had he kept that baby hair? What was his secret?

I turned to him and said, "I'm sorry I can't help you carry some of these boxes. I just got a manicure."

"You deserve it," he said.

I wanted to hug this man. I deserve it! I deserve it! "Thank you! Thank you!" I wanted to jump up and down. Can I take this man wherever I go? When I question if I deserve something or not, I can just ask him, knowing he'll say YES!

Compliment Number 3

I ran into the third complete complimentary stranger at Lowe's hardware store while I was roaming the aisles looking for a power cord. But I couldn't remember what they were called so I walked up to a chipper-looking salesman and asked, "Do you have that thing with a wire that has six outlets?"

"You mean a power cord?"

"Yes, that's it."

"You said that so cute," he said and laughed.

Is it possible to become addicted to compliments from complete strangers? I think so. I hope Compliment Number 4 comes soon. I don't know how much longer I can wait.

The Man with the Novel Voice

There was only one woman waiting at the doctor's office when I opened the door. She was petite, with the kind of sterling gray hair we all wish for in old age. She held a *Ladies' Home Journal* magazine close up to her nose and barely looked up as she saw me come into her line of vision.

I nodded hello. She barely acknowledged me. A few minutes of ensuing silence went by. She read and I flipped through torn magazines, noting several missing pages. I considered staring into my phone, but decided that the doctor's office desperately needed redecorating or should I say decorating, and began imagining it transformed, beginning with scarlet paint on the walls, a large oriental rug (even though I know doctor's offices never have them) and a variety of plants, three at least—a jade, a spider and a fern. I considered the time of day (2 p.m.) and the sun. A coffee table, that's what was fundamentally missing in this room. I weighed materials: Glass? No, not good for a doctor's office. Bamboo possibly, a…

Suddenly a large man wearing a white dress shirt and khaki pants opened the door. "Good afternoon, ladies," he said like he knew us. His bass voice was so powerful, it could have rearranged our chairs. "I hope you all are having a good day."

Do you mind," he said to Ms. Sterling Locks as he walked slowly toward an empty chair next to her, "if I sit here and look out the window for my mother?"

"No," she murmured, mesmerized by this man. She

pretended to keep reading, but I could tell she wasn't. Her magazine had lowered ever so slightly. Not a page moved. Not a rustle was heard.

They need music too in this office, I thought. A little "Bubbly" by Colbie Caillat would help.

Then I turned and observed the man too, like a spy would; I didn't want him to think I was staring. He didn't move an inch as he continued looking out the window for his mother, as if it were the only job in the world.

He treated the doctor's unattractive waiting room like someone's home. I respected him for that. Somehow he had learned you don't enter a space without greeting the people in it, whether they are strangers or not. And you don't sit next to people unless you ask their permission.

I was sure that he entered all spaces the same way and I wanted to ask him about it. Just as I was thinking about how to word my question, the nurse called my name. I gathered my handbag and stood up. I was glad I didn't have to wait any longer, but I did wish I could have seen how he greeted his mother. I imagined he fussed over her with that sonorous voice of his. Maybe he would even sing to her. What a lucky woman.

An Un-Unencounter

Standing close behind me in line at the hardware store was a willowy woman with a cordial smile and eyes that anchored on the cashier and me as if she had something to share. Before I could put my wallet away, she jumped in, asking the cashier and me, "Do you know what a ReadeREST is?"

"I was watching 'Shark Tank' and I found out about this," she went on. "I just got it in the mail today."

She pointed to the narrow, silver device she was wearing on the collar of her robin's egg blue oxford shirt. "You see," she said, "it's for your reading glasses so you don't need to buy an eyeglass necklace. You put it on like this." She demonstrated by detaching and reattaching the magnetic clip. "Isn't that great?"

I was actually in a hurry, but if people want to talk with me in this day and age of what I call the "unencounter" (i.e., the disconnect from real people when in their presence), I listen if I possibly can.

"I like it," I said, "but I'd be worried that I'd forget that it was on my shirt and it would end up in the washing machine."

"I'm not worried about that," she said, beaming, and hung her glasses back over the ReadeREST.

I doubt I will ever buy a ReadeREST, but it was good to see someone so excited about something that she wanted to share about it with everyone she saw. Whatever it takes to connect with someone, I thought. That's what counts.

STRANGERS IN THE NEWS

Meet-Up in the Ball Pit

Remember when you were a child and you went down slides for hours with kids that you just met at the park? You instantly bonded with them over who could go the fastest. One of Oprah's Super Soul Sunday segments was about an urban area ball pit created by SOULPANCAKE's Devon and Golriz to bring out the kid in passersby.

Devon and Golriz's purpose in building the pit was to create a place where adults who don't know each other can get together and discover connections between themselves. Each ball has a question on it that is used as a conversation starter.

It was just a hoot to watch a young man and woman on SOULPANCAKE's video discover that they both have missing teeth. Seeing these random strangers discover something they had in common was very moving.

Every city, town, and suburb should have a meet-up ball pit. It just screams fun, beckoning you to jump on in and enjoy yourself. Let your worries go, and make a connection with someone new.

An Encounter with a Stranger Can Glisten Like Pearls

How is it that the briefest connections in our lives can sometimes be the most important ones?

That's a theme I've been thinking about lately. I realized that if I hadn't said hello many years ago to an attractive and distinguished stranger, I would never have met my husband. We often have only seconds to make a decision about whether we want to connect with someone.

You could argue that any particular connection is—or isn't—meant to be, that these moments hang on fate, or grace, or some other force outside you. Or you could argue that each of us has tremendous power to affect the quality of our own lives—and the lives of others—and that making the choice to step out of your comfort zone to speak to a stranger can frequently change your life for the better.

The more I thought about this theme, the more I began to wonder how attitudes about relating to strangers have changed over time. And that made me curious to see if stories about encounters with strangers were reported in the news back in 19th century America.

As I searched for newspaper articles, I discovered that they certainly were. Many different journalists wrote many types of stranger stories. This particular one spoke to me and made me smile. I think it will make you smile, too. It's a beautiful story called "Strange but True" about a beggar who asked a stranger for money—and created a whole new, abundant life for himself by making this encounter one of genuine connection.

"Strange but True" was written for the *Detroit Free Press* and was reprinted in the *Milwaukee Sentinel* on October 2, 1899. Notice its charming, descriptive details and language:

Strange but True

Detroit Free Press: The glare of the electric lights made the rain drops glisten like pearls. Cabs rumbled over the pavements and cable cars whirred by. Nearly everyone had gone inside somewhere.

By the way, this was in Chicago. A man plodded along State Street in the rain.

He was making for the Palmer house. In front of him, no one could see more than his legs, for he held his umbrella low before the face of the storm.

A shabbily dressed young man stepped out from a doorway and fell into step with the man carrying the umbrella. "Mister," he said, "can't you give me a little bit o' money to help get a bed? I only want a little: can't you, mister?"

The man with the umbrella stopped, reached into his pocket and drew out a coin that he handed over to the young man. Then he proceeded along State Street.

He was about to turn into his hotel when a hand rested on his arm. He looked around. It was the same young fellow who had begged a coin a few moments before.

"Well, what do you want now?"asked the man.

"I just wanted to give this back to you," was the reply of the younger, as he drew his hand out of his pocket. "I guess you thought you gave me a quarter. See, it is a $5 gold piece."

The man with the umbrella looked at the palm of the hand held up to him. In its center lay a $5 gold piece, and he remembered that he had had one in his pocket.

He took it from the beggar and said, "Come in here with me." He sought the manager of his hotel and secured a position in the office for the young man. Today that young man is secretary of a certain parquet flooring company of Chicago.

There is no particular moral to this tale, because it is true.

The Milwaukee Sentinel. (Milwaukee, WI) Monday, October 02,1899; pg. 4; col. D

Stranger in the Attic

Have you seen the documentary *Finding Vivian Maier*? It's a fascinating film. Vivian was a street photographer in New York and Chicago in the 50s and 60s who took thousands and thousands of pictures of ordinary people, animals, and objects. She had the uncanny ability to capture them in moments of intense beauty or tragedy. But no one knew of her—or her extraordinary talent—during her life, only after her death when a Chicago historian, John Maloof, bought some of her photos at a storage facility's auction.

Maloof was so impressed with her work that he went on a search to discover more about her. He found that Vivian Maier was not only a photographer—her income came from her work as a live-in nanny for several different households on the affluent North Shore of Chicago. When he began contacting the families she'd worked for, he learned that none of her employers seemed to know much about her. They had never even asked to see the pictures she took of their own children.

One of the disturbing moments in the documentary is when viewers see that Vivian was taking pictures of a boy in her care right after he was hit by a car while the boy's family was standing in the road next to him. The mother clearly saw her son's nanny shooting photo after photo of the accident scene, but never confronted her about it.

Through Maloof's extensive interviews with the now-grown children who were in Vivian's care and their parents she worked for, *Finding Vivian Maier* raises questions about people's self-absorption and their inability to see what they don't want to see. Some of her employers even indulged her odd habits, like collecting old newspapers, knowing that she'd never get rid of them. She had so many piles of papers that her bedroom floor sagged and she could barely walk through the room.

She even requested that her employers put a padlock on her bedroom door and never enter it, and they obliged her. Did they ever wonder whether their children were safe with Vivian? Were they that desperate for someone to care for their children that they were willing to turn a blind eye? In retrospect, who was stranger—Vivian or her employers?

The Hermit of North Pond, Maine

What would you ask a hermit if you met one? I wondered about this when I read an article in *The New York Times* about Christopher Knight, 47, a hermit who lived under a tarp in the Belgrade Lakes area of Central Maine for 27 years. He went from the woods to the Kennebec County Jail because it turns out he was not only a hermit, but also a hermit-burglar who admitted to committing at least 1,000 burglaries, from batteries to bacon to books.

At first, I was surprised to hear that Christopher had "captured the imagination of people from around the world, who began sending him bail money and even marriage proposals." But now I get it. I'm intrigued by his story, too. People love legends and Christopher plays into a lot of people's fantasies: living off the grid without paying taxes, living a life of freedom, living on his own terms—no boss, no need to get up early and go to work. No bothersome phone calls, texts, tweets or emails.

According to the article, when Christopher was caught, "He told the police that he had not spoken during his decades of self-exile except for one day in the 1990s when he had uttered a greeting to a passing hiker."

His interaction with the hiker really stood out to me because it represented the only moment of human conversation he had had in close to three decades. How does someone not talk with another human for so long? Did Christopher talk to himself? I wondered. When the hiker walked away, did Christopher feel a sense of loss that he had missed the opportunity to connect?

Christopher's exchange with the hiker made me think
of questions I'd like to ask him. As I wrote the questions
down, more began to emerge.

> Were you ever in love?
> Did you ever write letters to family or old friends
> and wish you had mailed them?
> Did you have any old photos with you?
> When you were growing up, did you dream of
> becoming a hermit?

I tried to picture this strange "Boo Radley of the Woods"
in jail. He went from living in a beautiful green world to a
dismal gray one, overpopulated and noisy. He chose to do
what he did to survive the wilderness and that led him to
where he is now—locked in a place full of people where he
must also learn to survive.

For the Love of People

A friend of my daughter's told me about a website called "Humans of New York." She knows that I write a blog about strangers and she thought I would be interested in Brandon Stanton's work. To me, he's like a comrade out in the world and, while we might never meet, we are in the same field. We have an intense interest in capturing the details of others' lives and sharing about them.

Brandon had been a bond trader in Chicago before moving to New York with a camera and a goal to "set out to photograph 10,000 New Yorkers and plot their photographs on a map." That was his plan when he began, but his project gradually took on a life of its own and soon he was collecting quotes that people told him as well as short stories they shared about themselves.

Due to his vision he now has over fourteen million likes on Facebook. He told the *Huffington Post* when they interviewed him: "A lot of times I ask these people very personal questions and they'll answer. They'll tell me everything because a lot of times I'm the only one who's ever asked. I can tell when I talk to them—eight million people in this city, and nobody's ever asked about their life."

In another interview he talked about how it isn't always easy to photograph someone because sometimes they don't want to be photographed. When that happens he just deals with it and goes on to the next person.

I do the same. There are more people who want to connect than those who don't. Like Brandon, I've learned that there are many people who would like to talk about their lives if someone would just listen.

The Heartwarming Story of a Fuzzy Bear's Travels

On December 10, 1994, there was an article by Michael T. Kaufman in *The New York Times* about how Ms. Dollinger's second-grade class from the Dalton School let Fudge, their class bear, out into the world, to be taken on a journey by strangers.

His adventures began on October 18th when the children left Fudge in a food shop—with a note and a journal. They asked that he be taken around to see the sights of New York and that his adventures be written down. They also wrote that they would like him to be left with responsible people. Lastly, they asked that Fudge be returned by the first week in December.

Some of the children worried that they'd never see him again. One girl named Jessie said, "I was worried that somebody who had him would not be very careful and would let him get very wet."

I would have worried about Fudge, too. That was a long time to entrust strangers to the care of a beloved bear. How would the children fare if he wasn't returned? What if he was returned, but with a missing limb—or worse?

Someone, however, did return Fudge to the Dalton school one December afternoon. According to *The New York Times* article, each of the children hugged him. I can't even imagine how happy and amazed they must have been that he made it back safely, all in one piece.

Ms. Dollinger read Fudge's journal to the class. It turned

out that fifteen people had taken him to their homes in different parts of the city. Fudge visited the Chrysler building with a woman who took him there on her bike. He saw the show *Stomp*. He went on a plane to Washington, and to St. Louis with people in the publishing business. He also visited a classroom with children that had emotional difficulties and became their friend.

In supposedly cold, impersonal New York City, various strangers willingly took care of a two-foot-tall stuffed bear and wrote about their experiences. Then they entrusted other strangers to show him more of their city. Just think about it, and let it into your heart—what fifteen people took it upon themselves to do for a class of second graders they would never meet.

What I Learned from a "Writer of Dark Fiction"

Now, I don't read dark fiction, and I had never heard of Harry Crews. But when I read a *New York Times* article back in March of 2012 with the headline, "Harry Crews, A Writer of Dark Fiction, Is Dead at 76," I was so intrigued by the way Crews used brightness to create the darkness in his work that I copied some of the words: "Young Harry loved stories, but there were few books to be had. Instead his narrative gifts took root in the Sears Roebuck catalogue. 'Things were so awful in the house that I'd fantasize about people in the catalogue,' he said…. 'They all looked so good and clean and perfect, and then I'd write little stories about them.'"

I love how Harry, who had so little material available to him, made do with what he had. Sometimes less is definitely more, and in Harry's case, this was true. Today, we seem to have the opposite problem. Instead of not enough "material", we have way too much: Instagram images, tweets, Facebook posts, email, and yes, even snail mail, keep coming at us.

The other day, jammed into my mailbox with a slew of other mail, was a 1.75-inch thick catalogue from Restoration Hardware. My first response was concern about the environment. I called them immediately to request that my name be removed from their list, and then dropped the catalogue into our recycle bin.

Then I remembered the words of that "Writer of Dark Fiction." Thanks, Harry. Maybe I don't want to remove myself from every catalogue list after all. Maybe I need to go out to the recycle bin and fetch me some stories.

STRANGERS YOU LEARN
SOMETHING FROM

Mrs. Pepper, Dangling Lemons and Directionally Challenged Rolls

When my daughter Olivia and I saw that an etiquette class was being offered at a nearby country club, we signed up. The purpose of the event was for students from different high schools to learn proper meal etiquette, along with a delicious four-course dinner at a bargain price.

The concept was that in the not-so-distant future, these young people would be interviewing for jobs and they were much more likely to be hired if their manners were impeccable.

The tables for six were randomly assigned, so we sat with a group of people that we didn't know—two lively pubescent boys in crisp white shirts and tan pants that kept laughing, a sophomore girl with her hair pulled up into a high, tight ponytail and her mother, who was lively and talkative.

Our lessons began as the soup was being served. I've broken the lessons down for you in case an etiquette class is not being offered at a country club near you and you are dying to know what you missed.

SALT AND PEPPER

Salt and pepper are married to each other. Did you know that? I salute you if you do.

In order to stress the importance of their marriage, I said aloud when passing the glass shakers to Olivia, "Here you go, Mr. Pepper, even though you might not want to go with your wife, even though you might need a break from her salty personality and a night out with the boys, you have to come along." And with that I clicked the shakers together and slid them to Olivia, who took them carefully from my hands and stood them side by side like soldiers on the table, which made us burst out laughing.

BREAD PLATES

Did you know that the only thing that goes on a bread plate is bread and butter? No, you cannot put an olive pit on a bread plate. If you have an olive pit, you must dispose of it ever so discreetly in your napkin, without anyone at your table noticing. How do you do it, you ask? Delicately, ever so delicately.

THE LEMON SLICE (OR WEDGE)

If there is a piece of lemon on your water glass and you don't like lemons, too bad. You still must pick it up and gently drop it in your water glass. Even if you hate lemons, suck it up. DO NOT, I REPEAT, DO NOT LEAVE A PIECE OF LEMON DANGLING ON THE EDGE OF YOUR GLASS. That is bad manners.

Who knew that this was such a no-no? Not the pubescent boys in their crisp white shirts, not the sophomore girl with the high tight ponytail, not even her mother, not my daughter. And yes, not even me.

THE BREAD BASKET

Did you know that rolls should always be passed counterclockwise?

The boys couldn't get this one "right" and kept passing the basket to their left until we all laughed ourselves silly.

Who invented this rule? I was so curious that when I got home I immediately did some online research and discovered that rolls are passed to the right because most people are right-handed. (Poor lefties.)

MAIN COURSE

Are you someone who saws at your meat? Do you cut the meat toward or away from you?

If you answer "no" to the first question and "toward" to the second, kudos to you. Your "knife manners" are impeccable. (If you're American, that is. The Europeans have different ideas.)

The two young boys at our table couldn't seem to figure out how to use their knives and forks properly. They were told to hold a piece of chicken with their forks and carefully cut the meat towards them, and not to use a saw-like motion. They couldn't get the hang of it, and the rest of us weren't doing such a great job either. It was another one of our etiquette bungles.

DESSERT

Be sure to eat your dessert with the utensil given to you for that purpose. No using your unused soup spoon or your already used dinner fork!

Clearly this lesson went unheeded by some: when dessert arrived, the boys used forks to eat their chocolate pudding. Oh dear. My daughter and I laughed so hard watching them that we had to spit our coffee into our napkins. The pony tail girl and her mom joined in our laughter.

Then I accidentally put my elbows on the table and we all roared. (Oh yeah! I forgot to tell you about elbow etiquette.)

Betting on Strangers

I'm not a gambler. Well, maybe I am. I don't hang out at casinos, but I do bid against strangers on eBay. And I do take risks—that the antiques I fall in love with are really what some person as close as Louisville or as far away as the Netherlands says that they are.

So far, I've only been swindled once, when I bid on a vintage purse that arrived with a funky smell. It was supposed to be from a smoke-free home, yet it not only reeked of smoke, but also of intensely sweet perfume that made me gag and some pungent chemical that the seller clearly had used to try to hide the other odors.

Unfortunately for the seller, I have a nose that should have been used for detective work, winemaking or perfumery. I inherited my keen olfactory sensitivity from my mother and I'm proud of it. Plus, it helped me get my money back for this misrepresented item—the resolution center at eBay took care of that.

I did learn a lesson from that noxious gamble. Some purchases are too intimate to make without smelling the item first. It's a strange thing to own a stranger's purse, to have numerous interactions with a previous owner through her lingering scent. Every time you take your lipstick out, you are reminded of what can never really belong to you.

The Parrot Lover from Brazil

December 21, Sarasota, Florida, 3000 block of Clark Avenue. Just before 5 p.m.

Sometimes if you pause for a minute you become a captive audience in a world of strangers. The pausing gives someone else a chance to speak.

So there I was sitting outside on a bench on which was painted an advertisement I didn't care to notice, waiting for my daughter Olivia. She had run into a convenience store to buy a cool drink.

I saw a petite, olive-skinned woman in her sixties with a crimson red scarf look at me and pause before she got into her white Ford Taurus. Was she looking at me or at someone in the window of the store behind me? It seemed like she wanted to say something, so I chose to help her by looking right back at her and giving her my full attention.

"Do you see the parrots over there between the trees?" she asked me. She pointed far away. It was an unusual remark from a stranger and it took me a minute to see what she was talking about. Then, I saw some distinct shapes on the telephone wires.

At first, I saw nothing special about them, but on closer inspection, and to my amazement, I saw by their hooked bills that they were indeed parrots. There were several groups of them, perched side by side as close as possible to each other.

"Yes, I see them," I said. Cars and trucks drove under them

41

in rush-hour oblivion.

"They mate for life," she said.

How romantic, I thought.

"If one dies, it's just terrible," she went on. "The other will kill itself by pulling its feathers out. I'm from Brazil, I know a lot about parrots."

"That's so sad," I said, picturing a lone parrot with just a few feathers left on its wing.

"It's beautiful up there, yes?" she asked me.

"Yes," I said.

She smiled at me, got into her car, quietly closed the door and started her engine.

I stared at the parrots...wild, in love on the telephone wire. I wouldn't have noticed them if she hadn't pointed them out.

Flasher

I'll admit it. I've been flashed.

I was fourteen years old, walking to my friend David's house on an early July morning, when a black, slightly beat-up Cadillac stopped in the middle of the road near where I lived. That's strange, I thought, a car stopping right there.

Then a man wearing a black trench coat got out of the car. I remember that he was facing away from me towards his car and that he had thin, hairy legs and bare feet. He paused in an unnatural pose. Before I could process what was happening, he turned towards me, opened his trench coat and revealed his privates.

I was shocked. Why is that man showing me his body? I don't want to see his body. I think I must have stood there frozen for a few moments, until he got back in his car and drove away. Not quickly, as you might imagine, but rather matter-of-factly.

I turned, and began running in horror towards my house. I passed the two-story stucco with the many concrete steps, ran stupidly through the alley, which was the shortcut home. There was no one around, no one to shout to: "There's a naked man! There's a naked man! There's a naked man!" I didn't think he was going to come after me and hurt me, but I didn't really know. It was so disturbing, so perplexing, so creepy. All these questions with no answers went through my mind. Nobody had ever told me about men who flash themselves to girls.

What I don't remember is what happened afterward.
Was there anyone at home when I got there? Did I tell
someone?

I can't say that this incident scarred me for life. But it
did teach me that a strange man can accost a teenage
girl walking to her friend's house on any ordinary day. I
became one of the many girls whose simple trust in the
world is taken away by a stranger with bad intentions. I
learned to be on guard, realizing that there are people out
there who are not well.

Sometimes I wonder if that man is still flashing, still
stepping out of his Cadillac to shock unsuspecting teenage
girls. Hopefully he's stopped—or been stopped. Hopefully
he has some remorse for the wrongs he has done.

Thirty Minutes in the Life of a Volunteer Reading Tutor

Today I met my match in a wispy thin girl with tiny, pale wrists. As a volunteer reading tutor, you never know on any given day who you will tutor. Hopefully, you will have the same child or children many times, so that you will see progress, or better yet, success in their reading. Yet, this may not happen, and what you have to say to yourself when you enter the door of the school where you volunteer is, How can I be of service to whomever needs me today?

Before I got to my desk I noticed that Marcus, the boy I usually tutor, had failed to show up. When I asked his friend Trey if he knew where he was, he just shrugged his shoulders and said, "Sometimes, Markus just doesn't come to school. I don't know why." I would never have been allowed to do that, I thought, and I was grateful to my parents for not giving me that option. I walked into Mrs. Banner's third grade classroom, paused at the door and asked her, "Who needs help? Marcus isn't here today."

About five kids raised their hands. Some I knew had tutors and some probably didn't. Some of them didn't need a tutor. Mrs. Banner picked a girl who did not raise her hand. "Joanna, you go with Mrs. Schwartz."

That's funny, I thought. I had never seen a student picked who had not raised a hand. That should have been a red flag for me. This small girl grabbed a book under her desk and began walking toward me. I noticed that her uniform looked very neat. Her white polo had no dirt on it and her blue pants weren't frayed. That was unusual around here.

"I'm not really Joanna," she said to me while sitting down at the large table we were about to share. "I'm Jackie."

"Mrs. Banner," she went on, "always gets confused and thinks I'm Joanna, so I just go along with it."

She went on, "Joanna, of course, needs to do a certain amount of hours at school, so I came for her. Essentially, I'm taking her place."

I must have been sitting there with my mouth open. I took a deep breath and tried to process the all of it. I had been tutoring for four years and had yet to meet a child so articulate. I was sure I was dealing with a gifted one. She looked at me quite seriously.

My mind was racing. How long had Jackie pretended to be Joanna? And when was the real Joanna going to step forward? Were they twins or Irish twins? How dumb is this school? She picked up her Curious George Rides a Bike and announced, "I am now going to take a quiz for Joanna."

"Hey, Jackie, Joanna, or whoever you are," I said. "I think this has gone too far. You cannot take a quiz for someone else. That's called cheating and it's totally unacceptable."

She tilted her head slightly to the right as if to say, I never thought of that before. She paused, then said, "Now that you mention it, it could be a problem."

I said to her, "Why don't you come with me?" I was completely flabbergasted. I had not met a child this precocious since my own childhood. I didn't know what to do back then and I still didn't.

We walked over to Ms. Karen's desk. Ms. Karen runs the tutoring program. She is tall and thin and wears breezy blouses. "Did you know," I said, "that this is really Jackie, not Joanna? And she wants to take a quiz for her sister."

Ms. Karen's eyes narrowed and her jaw tightened. "Joanna," she said angrily, "Mrs. Schwartz is here to tutor you, not to hear your stories. Now go read your book and get back to business."

Oh, I thought. These are all stories she's made up. Well, what a creative young girl. Yes. I had been duped by a third-grader. I had tutored students who slept on floors. I had tutored students whose parents were in prison, but I had never tutored a liar, a brilliant liar at that.

Joanna and I quietly finished her Curious George book. I asked her if she played any instruments, because in the book George the monkey had swallowed a bugle.

"I play guitar, violin, drums, piano, French horn and bells," she said, "and I write songs."

School must be such a boring place for her, I thought. She clearly lived a full life in her head. I excused myself a moment and left Joanna with a pencil and paper. "Why don't you take a break," I told her. "You can draw something if you like." I walked down the aisle past the other tutors.

Ms. Karen waved me over. "She has a horrible home life," she whispered to me. "She now lives with her uncle."

"How sad."

I went back to the desk where she sat, looked at my watch and realized we were out of time. Turning toward her I said, "I enjoyed meeting you today. I hope I tutor you again." I realized that I had mixed feelings about the words that had just spilled out of my mouth.

She stood up, picked up her book and said nothing. Just when I thought she was going to walk away with no acknowledgment of our time together, she paused in the hallway and looked at me. She tilted her head slightly to the right in that same way again. Then she walked off toward the computers.

"I Never Buy Retail"

I was picking my way through some plastic bins of old kitchen utensils at a Sarasota thrift shop admiring the beauty of the handle of a vintage wooden spatula when I spotted her—an elegant woman, well into her seventies, in a large, Floridian straw hat, long black wide trousers and a red, vintage, beaded, Czech glass necklace.

She held a cream cardigan on a hanger, lifting it up towards the light to see if there were any spots. Then she smiled to herself, satisfied with her find, and placed it in her cart. As she started to wheel away, I thought, I bet she knows where all the great thrift stores are. So I walked up to her. "Do you know if there's a Goodwill store nearby that's a good one?"

"Yes, I do," she replied. Her brown eyes made me feel warm, like the Florida sunshine I was enjoying while away from my home in wintery Ohio. "I know where it is. I've been doing this for years. I never buy retail."

That's amazing, I thought. She never steps into Macy's, Walmart or Target. She finds everything she needs secondhand. Some people I know don't appreciate old things. Yet, so many of these items come from a time when quality reigned. They were built for beauty, and designed to last.

"It's good for the planet too," she added, as if she read my thoughts.

She looked in my cart. "You know that spatula you have? I love old utensils. I still have my mother's." She began to give me directions to the Goodwill and then said, "Why don't you follow me there? I'll show you the shortcut. I'm almost finished here."

"Sounds good," I said, happy to have found a thrifting companion.

When we walked outside, she got into an old white Cadillac with a handicap sign dangling from her mirror.

I followed her North on Tamiami towards the airport. Then I turned into the Goodwill parking lot and waited behind her for several minutes as she waited for an old man to pull out of a handicap spot. Relax, I said to myself. This is a woman who holds all the secrets. She knows there's no need to rush.

She stood waiting for me as I parked my car. Then the two of us followed a large crowd entering the store.

She pointed me toward the fashion jewelry. "They have some good jewelry here."

"Thanks," I said. "Good tip. I'm sure I'll see you in a few minutes."

She smiled.

A while later I spotted her in the housewares aisle. It was two days before Christmas and she had found three beautiful red velvet nesting boxes with gold ribbons in mint condition. They looked like they had once been used in a Christmas store display.

"And look at this," she said, holding up a snow globe with

a golden angel inside. It was beautiful. How did she find that? I wondered. She certainly had the touch.

"My friends and I are going to have a Christmas party!" she said. "Here, look what I found you."

I was so moved that she had been looking for something for me. She didn't even know me, but she had reached out to make me happy. She handed me a lovely white porcelain box with a silver-colored painted lid.

"You could put chocolates in it, or lots of things. Make sure to check inside. Just in case it's chipped." She gently pulled the tape off the lid and we both took a good look. It was perfect.

"That was so nice of you! I love it," I said. "Merry Christmas!"

"Merry Christmas!" she said and smiled at me, one bargain aficionado to another. Then she maneuvered her cart down the aisle towards the clothing department, back into the hunt.

Happy to Help?

Life be not so short but that there is
always time for courtesy.
~ Ralph Waldo Emerson

I'm in my neighborhood Target store struggling with a
medium-sized brown leather ottoman. I've gotten it off the
top shelf somehow, but like a bozo I have no plan for how
to get it into my cart, which already has a laundry hamper
in it. I look up and see another customer who's just entered
my aisle. For a moment I'm relieved: all I need is an extra
hand for a second, to make some room by folding up the
little compartment that you put babies or purses in.

"Hi, can you help me?" I ask. And I can tell in a flash she
wishes I hadn't seen her—that she was just about to dash
into another aisle and disappear.

She's clearly not happy I spoke to her, no doubt because
she knows helping me is the right thing to do but she
doesn't want to. I, on the other hand, don't like that I have
to ask her for help. I like to do things myself, which is
probably why I tried to get the silly ottoman into the cart
by myself in the first place.

She comes over to me with a frown on her face. "Can
you please lower that?" I ask as I point to the small seat
at the front of my cart with my elbow. She does as she is
asked, as if I'm the last straw in a string of miseries. Then
she hurries away without a word or even a look in my
direction.

It could be, I guess, that she's having a really bad day, or that something very upsetting is going on in her life. But the feeling I get is that she just didn't want to help me, or maybe anyone.

I pause in the aisle and consider the fact that you can learn an awful lot about human nature when you ask a stranger for help. Some people are genuinely helpful. It is their way to extend themselves. Others, like turtles, want to keep their heads in their shells and not get involved. Some are in between and come out to help when they feel like it.

I've read that one thing people of every culture have built into their DNA is the need for reciprocity, to repay an act of generosity. But maybe we have to be on the receiving end of courtesy before we can give it. Is it possible that no one has ever reached out a helpful hand to this woman? I hope, the next time she's in need, a total stranger offers to help without her even needing to ask.

What goes around comes around. This much I know.

Crossing Paths in
Johnny Appleseed Country

Sometimes your timing is all wrong and you cross paths with a stranger that, judging from the situation, you'd rather not run into. How you handle it will hopefully predict its outcome. This is not a time to hide your head in your cell phone or duck and turn away; no, it's time to "man up," or "woman up," as the saying goes.

I thought this was what was happening to me on a recent road trip when I pulled up to a gas station. My dog Louie had to go to the bathroom. As I walked him towards a grassy area, I noticed a lawn mower running with no one on it. Scanning the property, I saw the lawn mower man, who was stocky with fair skin and a reddish-grayish beard, picking up garbage from the grass. Oh, I thought, he's probably in a pisser mood. Why did that man have to be there right now?

"Hi," I said to him in my friendliest voice as Louie was just about to go. "I brought a bag. I'm cleaning up after him." I was wondering what his reaction would be. But he surprised me.

"I don't care about that," he said. "I care about the litter. You know what, people just don't care anymore. They just don't." He held up the clear garbage bag for me to see. Paper cups, candy wrappers, and napkins stared back at me.

"You know what I'm most proud of?" he said. "I'm most proud of my two kids. They both care."

"That's great," I said. "That's saying a lot. Maybe people would clean up more if they knew how lucky they were to live in this country. I know we're not perfect, but we have it better than most."

"You know what," he said. "I worked with a guy at the factory. I don't work there anymore, but he was from Madagascar. Every day he would say to me, 'I am so lucky to live in America. I am so lucky.' His saying that to me every day made me realize how lucky I was, too."

He paused. We looked at each other as he held the dirty bag.

I smiled at him. Memories of my Nana and Papa who immigrated to America from Russia came over me. I visited them weekly throughout out my childhood and there wasn't a day that I can remember when one of them didn't say to me, "You are so lucky to be an American. Never forget." And I never did.

The lawn mower man and I wished each other a good day, and we meant it. Then I deposited the poop bag in the trash can next to my car and drove away.

I don't know his name. He doesn't know mine, but it was good for both of us to meet, to be reminded that amongst the litterers lie the true Americans, ones who will carry their garbage as far as it takes until they find the right container.

Our paths had crossed on a strip of grass at a gas station near Mansfield, Ohio, a town where John Chapman, known as Johnny Appleseed, lived for 20 years, striving to leave the world a better place than he found it. And in that crossing we had both been awakened by memories of important role models in our lives, voices that speak to us, reminding us to respect our land, to throw things away in their proper place, and to go that extra mile in gratefulness.

STRANGERS HELPING STRANGERS

Sidewalk Hero

This story is dedicated to a stranger that I want to thank. He's my favorite stranger.

When I was twelve years old, I got a new, shiny-orange Schwinn ten-speed bike for my birthday. I remember the orange tape on the handlebars, wrapped up so perfectly, like it was yesterday. I was so happy to own something that was so cool.

One early morning just a few days later, I was riding through downtown Evanston, a few miles from my house. I was thinking of going to the bakery when I heard some threatening voices. "Stop, give us your bike."

"Give it to us now," another voice demanded.

I turned and looked over my right shoulder and I saw a group of teen boys in the distance, running towards me. I was scared out of my mind. I started pedaling faster and faster. They were getting closer and closer and I was losing control. I had no idea who the boys were.

Soon after I made a quick turn at the corner, I hit a crack in the sidewalk and the bike fell out from under me, smashing my knee and elbow on the concrete. I landed smack right next to a big man with a shaggy haircut like David Cassidy's. He looked very concerned. "Are you okay, are you okay?" he asked.

"They're coming, they're coming," is all I could say, tears rolling down my face.

I looked at my handlebars that were now twisted in a funny way and at my bleeding right knee, and then I saw those boys coming. What were they going to do to me?

But the David Cassidy man stayed next to me as I lay on the sidewalk holding my knees in pain. His arms were boldly crossed. I realized he wasn't afraid of those boys. They were punks to him. He stood there and glared them down.

"Let's get out of here," I heard one of them say when they saw the man ready to fight them if need be. The other boys turned quickly to follow their leader away and ran in the opposite direction.

"They're gone," the man said, helping me up.

I don't know how long he stayed with me, or what he else he said. I don't even know if I thanked him, I was so shaken up. But after a while, I got on my bike and rode home somehow, even though my new bike with its now bent-up handlebars and frame didn't work very well anymore.

I kept looking over my shoulder the whole way. I could hear those boys running behind me, but they weren't there.

Such lightness and such darkness happened on that day. I learned that people who are bad will hurt you to get something that they want. I also learned that people who are good are out there to help you.

"I'm No Angel"

When you've just gone into a ditch on the San Diego County freeway, Thomas Weller is the stranger that you'll wish for. He cruises the freeway looking for people who need help and he doesn't get paid a cent for it.

NPR featured him on StoryCorps on September 13, 2013 and his story was so inspiring that it moved me to tears. Weller knows how important a stranger can be in a person's life.

His dedication to others began with his own harrowing story. His mother told him not to drive his car during a blizzard but he did it anyway and ended up in a snow bank. If it hadn't been for a kind stranger that stopped to help him, he says, he would have frozen to death. That was back in 1964. He's been called an "angel" countless times by many of the people he's reached out to. He doesn't consider himself one, but I do.

Almost Heaven, One Tire at a Time

A little kindness from strangers can feel like a little piece of heaven. I received a large piece last week as I traveled through—where else? —Wild, Wonderful West Virginia on my way back home to Cincinnati. I got a flat on the West Virginia Turnpike and had to call my motor club, and then spent a night in Beckley since all the tire repair shops were closed.

The next day when I got to the tire shop and saw a swarm of people outside—and more inside sitting on some old beat-up couches—I knew it would be a while. Wow, I thought, I hope this is a good shop because I'm kind of stuck here.

I only had to wait about forty-five minutes, much less time than I expected. Then, the man at the counter in the blue and green plaid flannel shirt said, "Yeah, we got your tire fixed. It had a nail in it."

"What do I owe you?" I asked.

"Don't worry about it," he said. "Just a little West Virginia kindness."

I couldn't believe how nice he was. "Thank you so much," I said. "I really appreciate it."

I paused and reflected as I walked to my car. Thanks for making me feel like I'm home, I thought.

I've only spent a little time in West Virginia. It's beautiful and I've loved its mountains since the first time I saw them. Now I love the people. As John Denver's song goes, "Almost heaven, West Virginia, Blue Ridge Mountains... take me home."

Starbucks Grande

Last week a man I didn't know on Monday bought me a cup of coffee on Tuesday.

I walked into the weeklong class we were both taking and he said, "This is for you" as he smiled and placed it on the desk in front of me. It was a Starbucks Grande. I loved that it was a Grande; there was something extra special in that gesture. I rarely indulge in a coffee that size.

I thought his name was George but I had to glance at his nametag to make sure. "Thank you, George," I said. "What a nice way to start my day."

George was well into his eighties, with a round belly and a New York accent. He had a wonderful sense of humor, and the day before the two of us had laughed together at the same funny things our teacher said.

I gazed at my coffee and wondered what I could bring George the next day. I thought of donuts, croissants, cinnamon buns, even a bagel. I wondered if I should bake something instead of buying it. I finally decided I would bring him a KIND bar, probably dark chocolate cherry.

When I got to class Wednesday with George's KIND bar in my purse, he wasn't there. I was disappointed. Then I realized that, while I couldn't give back to George, I could give to someone else, someone I barely know. George's gesture was much bigger than the two of us. George had gifted me, I will pass his gift on, and…who knows how many people will be getting and giving an unexpected treat because of his unexpected Starbucks Grande?

63

It's funny, but years from now I probably won't remember what I learned in that class. But I know I'll remember George.

I Don't Know You, But Thanks for Opening the Door

The rain was coming down so heavily on my windshield that I knew I would get soaked when I made my run for it into the restaurant, whether I had an umbrella or not. I was feeling kind of dreary, rain-induced dreary.

Soaked, I stood at the entrance of The Original Pancake House and tried without success to close my shocking pink umbrella. The glass door to the restaurant looked dark and unwelcoming and I couldn't see through it. Suddenly it swung open. A good-looking man in his twenties with straight, dusty blond hair, faded jeans, and a gray t-shirt was holding the entry door for me. Then, before I could say, "Thanks," he dashed to the inside door to open that as well, stretching one work-booted foot back against the first door while stretching an arm across to hold the other one open. He was really giving it his all. His three co-workers, also in gray t-shirts and jeans, laughed at his antics.

"You made my day," I said to him, smiling as I walked through one open door and then the other. He seemed a bit surprised that he made me that happy, but he smiled back.

This, I think, is a man who often commits random acts of kindness. Even silly kindnesses. That made it even more fun, and I knew many people had benefitted from his goodness. The world is a better place because of him. Suddenly, my day was better; my mood no longer matched the dark gray sky.

Hannah Brencher—
The Love Letter Writer

I'm always looking for stranger stories and loved coming across a woman, Hannah Brencher, whose profession is to write love letters to strangers. What I love about her story is that she followed her heart and it led her to an interesting career cheering people up. How fun it must be to find one of her letters, let's say on your chair at Starbucks. Her goodness has spread and now she has a team of volunteers that write love letters.

Her journey began when she was living in New York City after she finished college. She felt lonely and fell into a deep depression. The way she handled her depression is extraordinary. She decided to write "love letters" to strangers. In the process she not only felt better, but she realized what she wanted to do with her life. She pointed out that in her generation, there are many people who have never received a letter. "It's a paperless world," she said.

I'm inspired by people like Hannah who follow their hearts, not always sure where it will lead them, but taking the risk anyway.

A Story of True Courage

I recently heard about an organization called the Jewish Foundation for the Righteous, whose mission is to support the many non-Jews who risked their lives to rescue Jews during the Holocaust. I went to the foundation's website (http://www.jfr.org) and stared in awe at the faces and stories of seemingly ordinary people who were, in fact, not ordinary at all.

How to pick one story to tell from so many inspiring ones is not an easy task, but something caught my imagination when I read about the Konochowicz family, from Poland. It was the word "stranger." The Konochowicz family did not know the two Jewish families they hid in their attic at all, yet they took care of them like their own.

The foundation's website shares these details: "The Silvermanns and Smuszkowiczes found shelter with the Konochowicz family, who were complete strangers. The family consisted of eight children, including 17-year-old Jadviga, the third oldest. The two Jewish families asked to stay for one night. They ended up staying for more than a year. Although the Konochowiczes were poor and barely able to care for their own family of ten, they provided food and shelter for the eight Jews."

There is a photo of Jadviga on the website. She's a pretty young woman with her long, blonde, wavy hair pulled back to show off delicate drop earrings. What was it like for her as a teenager, to live with the secret that there were two Jewish families hiding in her attic?

Perhaps she had a boyfriend who was never allowed in the

house. Maybe her friends weren't allowed in either. Or, if they were, she was probably afraid that one of them would hear a suspicious noise. She must have lived with the fear that her family would be caught and killed. She may have wondered if it was worth risking their lives to save the lives of others.

All the Konochowicz children probably had little to eat at times, and lay in their beds at night worrying about a knock on their door. But they learned a powerful message—their mother and father could not live with themselves if they let strangers die for no other reason than the fact that they were of a different faith.

Stories of courage like the Konochowicz's need to be told again and again to Jews and non-Jews alike, to remind people when they are feeling less than courageous that they are capable of so much more.

The Smiling Elephant, Part 1

Sometimes sitting in small restaurants with small tables very close to each other is a good thing. The Smiling Elephant Restaurant in Nashville is one of those small but special places. They serve, hands down, the best Thai food I've ever had. I didn't know that so many fascinating flavors could be found on one fork.

The customers are an eclectic mix of people including students, artists and families who love Thai food. Sitting next to my daughter Olivia and I was a girl with a double pierced nose and dyed black hair. The guy who sat across from her had pierced ears and short, choppy, rusty hair. Since it was my first time at this restaurant I wanted some advice on what to order. I turned to him just as his companion got a phone call. "What did you get? It looks delicious."

"It's the Cashew Chicken." He smiled. "It's really good."

"Thanks for the tip," I said.

Olivia and I looked around as a waiter and waitress delivered beautiful steaming dishes of rice paper rolls, dumplings and tall glasses of exotic Thai iced teas to other tables around us.

My Cashew Chicken arrived, along with Olivia's tofu vegetable dish. "This is delicious," we said at the same time.

As customers left the restaurant, some of them banged the gong that stood by the door to show their appreciation for their meals. It was their way of saying thank you, without words. I loved that idea of using an instrument to express feelings of gratitude. I think there should be gongs placed in spots all over cities and towns, so we can remind ourselves often how lucky we are.

Near the end of our dinner, I said to Olivia, "Oops, I need to take my vitamin. I almost forgot."

"Thanks for reminding me. I would have forgotten my vitamin too," said the young man who had advised me on what to order. He unfolded a small plastic bag from his coat pocket and popped the contents into his mouth.

"Anytime," I said. I thought it was charming that he had thanked me for reminding him to take his vitamin. I felt like his mother. I think I could have been. He was that much younger than me.

Olivia and I banged our gratitude with the gong on the way out. The Smiling Elephant had definitely smiled down on us.

MYSTICAL STRANGERS

The Smiling Elephant, Part 2

I forgot to tell you something about the Cashew Chicken Vitamin Man who sat next to me at The Smiling Elephant. When I told him my daughter and I lived in Cincinnati, he told me he went there all the time.

"Some of the most famous crystal healers in the world live in Cincinnati," he said. "I go to the workshops. I'm a crystal healer."

I was a bit surprised. Cincinnati was ground zero for crystal healers? "Well," I said, "I didn't know that."

"Yeah, I'm there a lot."

You know how, when you meet someone from a different city, you think you're never going to see them again? I realized now that I might see this stranger again—not at a crystal healing workshop, because I wasn't planning on going to one, but maybe at another Thai restaurant, this time in my hometown.

Meeting him reminded me that there is serendipity everywhere. We are all connected in some way, whatever our beliefs, pastimes and passions.

When I got back to Cincinnati and sat down at my desk, I noticed the amethyst crystal that I had placed in a short, fluted vase a few years ago. I picked it up and gazed at it, resting in the palm of my hand—dusty, but still beautiful.

How old is this crystal? I wondered. I turned it over and felt the rugged bottom. What part of the world does it come from?

I had bought it for its beauty and sparkle, but in doing a bit of research I discovered that its purpose is to promote harmony and balance, to calm the mind and offer self-healing. Amethyst is even known to strengthen the immune system.

In honor of the healer at The Smiling Elephant, I carried the crystal to the laundry room sink and ran warm water over it, watching it regain its original, exquisite clarity.

Broken Blue

A few years ago, on a spring day, a petite woman wearing a breezy white cotton skirt and blouse joined our writing class. She wore a long gold necklace with a tiny charm of a green-enameled hummingbird in flight. On her lap she placed a neat stack of small, recycled tan paper journals.

When it was her turn to read, she chose a story about the joy and sadness she felt in seeing a tiny, blue, broken robin's egg on the sidewalk near her home.

We were so engrossed in her story that we listened like children do, wide-eyed and speechless. We were all there with her looking at this tiny egg lying on the uneven concrete. She described to us what it meant for her to find it, all the beauty, and the anxiety she had felt. When she was finished reading, there was a long silence and then we all took a deep breath. It was a spiritual moment for us— we had strongly connected with the natural world through her writing.

A few days later, while walking my dog in a park, I was reminded of her when I too saw a cracked blue robin's egg lying on the ground. I bent down closer to inspect it and was mesmerized by its color, almost like the blue in a baby's eyes, but deeper. It was a mesmerizing hue only a robin could truly duplicate.

Every time this earthy woman came to our class she had more stories to tell of Mother Nature and her profound connection to her.

As I sit in the kitchen remembering her, a ruby-throated

hummingbird is sipping out of our bright red backyard feeder. It's the tiniest bird on earth and I'm endlessly amazed when I see one hovering in mid-air.

I would love to see a hummingbird's nest, those eggs as small as peas intact and waiting to hatch, but for now I'm happy just seeing this one tiny bird with its radiant wings beating eighty times per second. Because of one writer, I am now paying much more attention to the wonders around me.

MELISSA KOTLER SCHWARTZ

Down on Your Luck,
Wish for a Red Fox

The sky was that beautiful soft early morning shade of diffused blue; the air was cool; the grass was wet and green, so green it almost appeared artificial as I walked my dog. A robin flew by—and then I saw him.

He looked at me. I looked at him. I felt that timeless sensation of wonder, that wishing that a particular moment will last, all the while knowing it's not going to. The fox paused, blessed me and darted across the street into the woods.

The Welsh believe that if you sight a red fox, you are blessed with good luck. A surge of happiness came over me, and I crossed the street and peered into the stillness, hoping for another glimpse. But nothing spoke to me but the dense tall trees and crisp leaves that moved and whispered in the wind. Where was the fox? It was probably there, watching me, but I would never know.

Being human, questions visited me. When would I find out what my good luck would be? How long would I have to wait?

In the meantime, I had to finish my walk. As I headed up the hill, I remembered reading somewhere that the red fox appears to remind you to continue to pursue your goals. "I will honor that, Mr. Fox," I said.

What else did he want to tell me? I will just have to wait and see.

Transported in Time

An unlit oil lamp sits in the empty fire pit along with a small statue of a seated Native American man. Several people have come to hear Paul Leone, the storyteller, at the Mabel Powers Fire Circle at Chautauqua Institution in Western New York, on this hot July afternoon. They walk up and take their seats on two circles of benches. Large trees tower over them, shading them from the sun. Camper boys play in the ravine, looking for rocks. Some people use their pamphlets as fans.

Then Paul begins to tell his Native American stories and we are all transported to a time when the lines between modern and ancient, between people and animals, blur. For long moments we are all with him imagining the bear and the turtle, until a lawn mower starts up and we're snapped back to the here and now.

It's Nothing but an Evil Eye

What I remember about Western Turkey is not the Temple of Artemis, the Church of Mary or the Basilica of St. John, but a Turkish man in his fifties with a thick mustache at an outdoor market filled with colorful cotton clothes.

I was eighteen years old, looking at gauzy dresses on a rack outside. They were swaying ever so slightly in the wind and the sun felt sharp and hot on my back. The more I looked at the clothes, the more I felt engulfed in them, as if I couldn't escape.

Suddenly, there was a man standing right next to me. I had no idea how he got there. He reached out and took my hand and walked me towards a nearby shop. I remember shadows crossing a beige stucco wall where the sun was trying desperately to get in.

I was afraid. Where was my mom? Should I scream out? Something told me not to, that this man was not a threat.

He led me inside a store filled with clothes and jewelry, sat me down and revealed what was in his left palm—a small silver hand with a deep blue jeweled eye in the middle.

I had never seen anything like it before. A chill went down my spine as I stared at this charm dangling from its silver chain. Why was he showing me this?

"This is an evil eye. It will protect you," he said with certainty in his voice.

I took a deep breath, secure in the knowledge that this

man, a stranger, had wanted to protect me. I didn't understand why, but he pressed the evil eye into the palm of my hand. He then stood up and beckoned me to follow him back out of the store. I'll never know why he gave that gift to me. Maybe he was just being kind?

I kept it all these years and not long ago, I gave it to my daughter Olivia. She wears it from time to time. It's a bit big on her as it was on me when I was a young woman. Sometimes she asks me to tell her again the story of the man who gave me the evil eye.

Guardian Angel

Not long ago, I bumped into an acquaintance in the produce section of the grocery store. She looked drained, as if she had gone through something very difficult. I asked how she was and she began to tell me how she had miscarried a couple weeks ago.

"Oh," I said. "I'm so sorry to hear that."

She nodded. "After I saw my doctor at the hospital I was so upset," she said, "that I leaned against the hallway wall for support. I was crouching and sobbing. Suddenly, a woman who looked like a grandma came over to me. I don't know where she came from. She hugged me without saying a word. I cried on her shoulder for a minute. Then she stood up and left. I'm not sure she was real, but does it matter? She was there for me when I needed her most."

I was silent for a moment, trying to imagine how you could not know if someone was real if she was hugging you, trying to picture what this grandma might have looked like. Short, grey, flyaway hair? Thin wire-rimmed glasses resting gently on the end of her nose? Wearing her own handmade fuzzy powder-blue and white sweater? A wise woman archetype, I thought.

I've never had this experience, and I can't think of anyone else who has. But that doesn't mean it wasn't real. This acquaintance has always seemed very grounded to me. Who am I to say that there aren't guardian angels or other spiritual beings who appear in a crisis to help if no one steps forward?

"I don't think it matters if she was real or not real," I said. "Sometimes, the people who help us aren't whom we would expect."

The Waving Man

An elegant black man in his seventies used to live a few blocks away from my home in Cincinnati. He was tall and thin, with a wrinkled forehead, and always wore a dark suit. I called him The Waving Man because he and I waved at each other almost every day for seven years.

I took great comfort in seeing him. To me, he symbolized community—the community I longed for, a relic of the past. Since I had moved from Chicago, the feeling of being an outsider would crop up every once in a while and I would be reminded that this new city was not my hometown.

The Waving Man lived across the street from an old white wooden church. On almost any given day in reasonable weather, he would sit on the front porch of his small Victorian home with the peeling paint and wave from his chair at anyone who drove by. It was important to him, this waving. It was like a calling. You could see it in his eyes.

The road he lived on was a quiet one. One day I saw him wave to someone in a car behind me. The man did not wave back. Perhaps he thought that the elderly man was mistaking him for someone else. Perhaps he had the thought, Why should I wave back at a stranger?

My daughter Olivia and I did not see it this way. She was four years old the first time she saw The Waving Man, and she looked for him every day. Most of the time he was there, ready to greet and be greeted. I can still remember her small hand waving back and forth at him well after we had passed his house. I can still see her head turning back to catch his smile even after we had driven around the bend.

When The Waving Man wasn't there, Olivia worried about him. "Where's that man?" she'd ask.

"Maybe he's busy cooking, or reading a book," I'd say.

Often, the waving man was not alone on his porch. Sometimes an old woman, who I think lived there too, sat with him. Perhaps she was The Waving Man's wife, but she never waved. She glared at the passing cars. A young man, perhaps his grandson, would also appear from time to time on the porch. When The Waving Man waved and we waved back, the young man smiled at us.

One early spring, The Waving Man disappeared. A month or so went by with no sight of him, and his house seemed so lonely and vacant. The grass grew high. I thought maybe I should knock on the door and find out what happened to him, but I knew I never would. What would I say? "Hi, I'm looking for the man who waved at me for seven years."

I hope he's not dead, I thought with a feeling of dread. "Perhaps he's just out of town on an extended visit," I would say when Olivia asked about him. Day after day, I had to tell her that I didn't know when he might be back.

Then, one day in May, I drove by and saw the glaring woman. She was standing on the porch, looking like she wished her day would just hurry up and come to an end. Given the way she looked, I never expected to see The Waving Man again, but the next day, there he was, back in his chair on the porch. He looked as refined as ever, perhaps a bit thinner. He waved at me and I waved back more times than were necessary. Olivia watched me as she waved from the back seat.

"Maybe we'll meet that man one day," she said as I looked at her in the rearview mirror.

"Yes, maybe we will," I answered, though I didn't really think so.

But a few months later, after visiting my mother-in-law who lay dying in a Hospice facility, The Waving Man walked into a nearby Bob Evans restaurant where Olivia and I were having lunch.

"Look, Olivia," I said in a whisper, "it's The Waving Man."

We watched the hostess take him to a nearby booth. He sat down and took his napkin and carefully smoothed it on his lap with a graceful motion that reminded me of the kindness in his waves. That's when I realized why, after all the years of seeing him only on his porch, he had appeared here with us now, as Olivia and I were about to lose someone so special to us. He was waving goodbye to Olivia's grandmother.

Olivia and I stood up and walked over to him. "Hi," I said, "I'm Melissa." He looked at me, not as a stranger, but as an old friend.

"We've been waving at each other for a long time," I said. He smiled at me and reached for my hand. We held hands for a long time. He smiled at Olivia and patted her head.

"I'm Olivia," she said, smiling back at him.

"It's good to meet you. I've enjoyed waving at you," he said to her.

She blushed, but I knew she was pleased.

"I hope you all have a good lunch," he said. "It's good to know your neighbors."

"Thank you," I said. He had lifted our spirits once again, on a day we needed it more than ever.

Back at our table, Olivia sipped her milk in silence for a moment, then said, "We finally met him, Mama!"

"Yes, we did. Yes, we did," I said. But it seemed to me as if The Waving Man had known us all along.

The Lucky Cookie

Tonight our family had dinner at King Wok. Our waiter kindly gave us extra fortune cookies because we're regulars. When I opened mine, at first I couldn't believe my eyes. It said, "A short stranger will soon enter your life with blessings to share."

Pretty serendipitous fortune for someone with a blog called "Strangers I Have Known," wouldn't you say? Call it a coincidence, but I think not: I have been eating Chinese food and fortune cookies since I was in grade school and I have never seen this fortune before. I'm a believer in what they call the Law of Attraction, and this feels like a manifestation—that is, this particular fortune came to me because on some level I requested it.

YOUNG STRANGERS

A Perfect Circle

Sitting near young children when you're eating out can be a good or bad experience. Yesterday, at an Indian restaurant, we discovered that it was worth taking the risk. My husband, Steve, our son Sam and I chose a table next to a family with two small sons and a doting set of grandparents. One boy was about six years old and the other, who was in a high chair, looked to be almost two.

Of course the little toddler was the center of attention. He was seated with his back to us during lunch and happily munched on food that was passed his way. When he finished his meal, he lifted his arms for his dad to pick him up.

His wish was granted and his dad whisked him out of his highchair onto his lap. The boy took one look at our table and saw Sam. A big smile appeared across his face and got wider and wider. His cheeks got rosier and rosier. Then the giggles rose out of him, giggles that burst out like bubbles. He couldn't stop and Sam was smiling right back at him, his teen worries about the next day's math and science tests vanishing from his face.

An elderly couple in the corner booth who sat side by side comfortably but hadn't spoken a word to each other broke out in warm smiles as they watched the whole interaction in fascination.

The owner of the restaurant went over to the little boy's table and stood gazing at him, as if to say, Thank you for bringing such happiness to my restaurant. I can make good food, but joy like this I can't create.

"That's amazing," the little boy's father said to us, looking baffled at his son's gleeful encounter with a total stranger. "Jack just doesn't do that."

He kissed the top of Jack's head. "You have a gift," he said to Sam and Sam looked pleased.

"Yes, he does," I added. "Babies do react like that to Sam. He makes them laugh."

What a perfect circle: Sam made this toddler laugh, which in turn made Sam laugh. And watching the two of them together made the rest of us happy. There were smiles all around, thanks to this adorable little stranger.

Post Office: Roselawn, Ohio,
A Sunny August Afternoon after Lunch

Sometimes waiting in line has its benefits—it connects you to people in your community that you'd never meet. Today, I met a little girl named Vanessa and her grandmother. While a man behind me huffed and puffed and shuffled his feet in frustration over the wait, Vanessa, Grandma and I decided to make the best of the situation and talk to each other.

I said to the Grandma, "I think we're waiting for someone to get their passports."

She nodded. "I like your ring," she said.

Then Vanessa wanted to look at my ring, too. She held my hand gently to get a good look at it. It was a touching moment, a young girl gazing at a stranger's ring while holding on to her hand. And I have to say it made my afternoon. I'm not around little people enough and I can forget their innocent beauty.

"Vanessa, show the lady your ring," her grandma said.

Vanessa put her right hand out in a graceful gesture. There was a lovely silver ring with a tiny heart on her ring finger. "I love your silver ring," I told her. She smiled at me proudly and her big brown eyes got bigger.

She ran over to the little wooden bench up near the counter. I've always liked that the Roselawn Post Office keeps it there. I think it honors the little people of the world. Vanessa briefly listened to the conversation that was going on between the postal clerk and his customer and then tired of it.

She tapped her grandma's arm and motioned for her phone. Then, she tapped her grandma's arm again for her ear clip. She carried them both to the bench, where she placed the ear clip on her ear and tuned out the conversation between the clerk and the customer. She looked so grownup sitting on the bench with her legs crossed. Too bad, I thought, she's missing out on the opportunity that the front row offers her—a glimpse into the everyday world of people taking care of their business.

I wonder, when she grows up, if there'll still be a post office around where her children can sit on a little bench and listen.

A Splendid Summer Day

One summer day I was biking along in the idyllic small town of Chautauqua, New York, and I heard the shrill cries of a child nearby. The hysteria silenced all other sounds. As I got closer, I saw that the cries were coming from a boy about five years old with blond, cherubic curls spilling out of his red bicycle helmet. His face was smeared with tears.

Then I saw a white-haired man stop to ask him if he was okay.

"I lost my parents. I lost my parents," he sobbed.

"Don't worry," the man said. "I'll help you find them."

Thank goodness for this man, I thought. Talk about a guardian angel. The boy hadn't been alone for a second before a kind stranger came to his aid. But wait—what if the boy was afraid of this man he didn't know? What if his parents had taught him about "stranger danger," as well-meaning parents should? If so, he was in the midst of a true moral dilemma.

Suddenly I was worried about the man who was offering to help him. What if he was a pedophile? I hated to think such a thing, but unfortunately you never know. The media teaches parents to tell their children, if they are ever lost, to ask a woman for help. Now we all know that all women aren't good. Maybe the child's odds are just statistically better with a woman. Right then I decided I needed to help too, that this man should not be the only person in charge of this little boy. And just as I was thinking that, a young couple in their twenties also walked up to help.

I took a deep breath. What a relief, I thought, to see such a beautiful picture of kindness. Three strangers on a splendid summer day, stopping to help someone in need. Whatever plans they had had, wherever they were going before they discovered the lost boy, were on hold, because doing the right thing to help him was clearly the only choice they wanted to make.

Stranger in the Cabin

I was the one who noticed first. I couldn't find my favorite light blue t-shirt, the soft one I loved that had been washed a hundred times.

"Jamie, did you see my blue t-shirt?"

"No, but I'm sure you'll find it," she said.

I looked again in the drawers of the bureau that had been assigned to me, then under my bed. Where had I put it? I was mad at myself for losing it.

Then Jamie said, "I can't find my blue jeans. I only brought one pair." She was tossing things out of her suitcase onto the floor as she spoke.

I walked over to Jamie and together we stared into her bag. "My jeans were right here. I saw them last night," she said. We looked at each other, not knowing what to think. We knew everybody who had been in the cabin.

Then Kristen opened the door, startling us. "I forgot my sweatshirt. It's freezing out."

After looking for a minute, she said, "Hey, where is it? It was on the hook right here last night."

"We're missing stuff, too, Kristen," Jamie said, and looked out the window at the lake, as if it could tell her what was happening.

If this is a joke, I thought to myself, it isn't funny.

The next minute we were down on the floor looking under bunk beds, behind bunk beds, in drawers, drawers that weren't ours. We felt uncomfortable, but we did it anyway. Suddenly, Kristen piped up, "Oh, my gosh, my sweatshirt is in Tori's trunk."

"What?" Jamie and I said in unison. Kristen opened the trunk wide for us to see. There was our missing stuff, and other bunkmates' stuff as well. It was all just crammed in there. It was creepy how much of our stuff was in Tori's trunk.

The three of us stared at each other, speechless and scared. "What do we do?" Kristen finally asked.

We kept looking at each other. It seemed like time froze in that cold cabin.

"We ask her why," I said.

They nodded.

We then went about our business, getting ready for breakfast. Not knowing what to say to each other. We knew that something was wrong with Tori, we just didn't know what. We were trying to process what was happening. It was the 1970s; we were twelve years old. People didn't go around labeling people with types of mental illnesses back then. We'd never even heard the term "mental illness."

Just then, Tori opened the door to the cabin and walked in, oblivious to the fact that we were staring at her. She did not say hi.

"Why did you do it?" Jamie asked her.

"Do what?" Tori said, brushing aside her straight blonde bangs.

"You know, take our things?"

All I remember is Tori blushing a little bit and looking down with a smirk. There was no apology. She grabbed a small notebook off the bureau she shared with me and walked back out the screen door.

We all stood there silently for a long time. I remember getting goose bumps.

Then the three of us made our way toward the mess hall. Glad to have breakfast. Hoping to forget things. We didn't turn her in or tell any of the counselors.

Looking back, we may not have done her any favors by keeping silent. But we were only twelve years old, and we didn't know what to say, or how to say it. Something had shifted in all of us. We were touched by adult problems. The tide was coming in.

The Girl on the Rock

I had the oddest feeling yesterday when I opened a squeaky metal file in my basement storage room and looked through some old letters and notes, mostly from my junior high and high school years. I loved every minute of standing there, reading through bits and pieces of my life, remembering this and that, and not remembering that and this at all. I stood there until my feet hurt. Who was this person?

Then I found a "Camp Echo First Place" blue ribbon for swimming across the lake and back. I had no memory of swimming twice across the lake. No memory of the cold Michigan water or the boat with the lifeguards that must have watched us kids as we swam back and forth. I've always been a natural swimmer, but was never one to go long distances. Who was this thirteen-year-old girl that had taken that on? Where had she gone?

I looked further and found an old white box in a drawer. In it was another first place ribbon from Camp Echo, this one for "War Canoe." This baffled me even more. There are a lot of people needed to paddle a war canoe. Who were the kids who won with me and what did it feel like when we won? Did we have a huge celebration?

What had happened to my memory here? Why do we remember some things and not others? Why do some people remember our stories better than we do? I'd like to talk to those other campers, now adults, who were on that war canoe with me. "Do you remember?" I would ask them. "What was it like?" Inevitably, someone would remember.

97

It's funny what I do remember about those two weeks at Camp Echo some forty years ago. I have an image of lying in the bottom bunk. The mattress was thin and smelled of mildew and did not help my homesickness go away. I didn't tell anyone that I was homesick, although I'm sure I was not the only one. I just tried to be strong in the dark, whatever that meant. I had a lot of mixed feelings about being away from home.

I guess you could say I wasn't a camper. I didn't return to Camp Echo. Instead, I spent the rest of my childhood summers hanging out on the big grey rocks at the edge of Lake Michigan, where I grew up. Happiness to me was summers spent there with my friends, looking out at the water. We covered ourselves in baby oil to get tan. That was long before we knew about skin cancer.

I can remember the choppy waves and, on rough days, the danger and thrill of the water crashing and getting us wet. I can remember reading the painted words boyfriends and girlfriends wrote on the rocks for each other. I remember all us girls shouting like moms at the boys to "Be careful!" as they jumped from rock to rock.

No parents checked on us. We just hung out until we got tired or hungry. Those were the days and my memory of them is so clear that I can smell Lake Michigan now and hear the water swooshing hard at the edges of the rocks. I can smell the dead fish like they washed up yesterday, but it wasn't yesterday at all.

This much I know, we are strangers to ourselves sometimes. That's okay as long as we can find a piece of ourselves to take home. The memory of being with my friends on those rocks is a blessing to me, the closest I can come to a spiritual journey where nature, friendship and growing up all come together. Maybe I kept those memories because they're such beautiful ones.

For the Love of French Fries

The main draw at Boxcar Barney's in Mayville, New York, is ice cream, especially on hot summer afternoons like this one. When I walked up to order, the line had dwindled to two or three waiting customers, but I knew it would swell again shortly. I was happy that I got my food at just the right time.

Sitting at a picnic table in the shade, I reflected that this place was a little bit of heaven right here. Today it wasn't the Maple Walnut ice cream for me. It was a broiled hot dog wrapped in steaming tin foil with fries prepared to perfection. I watched the sailboats and motorboats on Chautauqua Lake.

Then I saw a big group of kids from a nearby day camp walking ever so quickly, almost running towards Boxcar Barney's. They had that look of kids on a mission. They had waited all afternoon for the end-of-their-day ice cream. They looked hot and tired. Ready to eat and go home.

I turned to the woman on the bench behind me. "I bet you're happy you got that ice cream when you did," I said, nodding toward the oncoming crowd.

"I sure am," she said. As we chatted, I learned that the young man sitting with her was her visiting grandson, who was going to college out on the West coast.

The three of us watched the campers as they walked up to place their orders. The most intriguing kid to me was a boy of about eleven. All the other campers went to stand in line, but he tossed his backpack down on the grass, made a place for himself, pulled out a hardback book, and began to read.

A few of the boys came and sat at my table after they had gotten their ice cream cones because there wasn't room anywhere else. I found it quite charming how they went about it. No one asked if they could sit with me, they just looked at me to see if I was okay and then quickly sat down and started talking with each other.

All of a sudden a boy about ten with flame-orange hair and matching freckles said to me, "Can I have your French fries?" He pointed to two of them that had fallen out of my cardboard food basket onto the table. I was about to act motherly and say to him that the fries might be unsanitary, sitting on the table like that, but then I decided that if he really wanted the two lone fries it wouldn't hurt him.

"Sure," I said. "You can have them."

"Thanks," he said, grinning. He gobbled them up so fast that I wanted to offer the rest of my fries to him, but that seemed like I'd be crossing the stranger line. The fries on the table were up for grabs. The fries on my plate had my stamp on them. Some of the boys looked at the French Fry Conqueror in amazement, like they wished that they had asked me for fries too.

My table-mates licked their ice cream really fast until it quickly disappeared and then chased each other around, roaring with laughter. Some of them even briefly stopped to visit with their book-reading friend.
Together the Grandma, her grandson and I just watched the campers, amused by their antics.
Suddenly, the French fry boy came up to me and said,

"Thanks," and reached his arms out to me and gave me a hug. I was so surprised that I had one of those did-that-just-happen reactions. It was really so charming of him to do. Such a small gesture on my part, forfeiting two lukewarm French fries, but to him it was a big deal.

I turned and looked at the Grandma and grandson. They were grinning from ear to ear, along with me and this exuberant, freckled, young stranger.

STRANGERS ON THE JOB

The Phlebotomist and Me

When I read an obituary and someone comments that the person who died "never met a stranger," I immediately admire him or her. To me this is a gift.

I've always believed that connecting with people who aren't a part of our lives is important because we are all in this together. We all share the same basic human needs and wants. Also, it's good to learn from others. And, most of the time, after I talk with someone I don't know, we both walk away with what Barbara Fredrickson, PhD, calls "micro-moments of shared positive emotion."

Nicole Frehsée explored this idea in an article in the February 2013 issue of *O, The Oprah Magazine*, "The Love Connection." Frehsée said, "Here's some simple advice: Spread the love. Not just with your partner, family and friends but with people you hardly know, because the more loving you are in everyday life, the healthier you could be."

I've taken this advice to heart for as long as I can remember. I talk to strangers all the time, like when I went for a blood test the other day. The phlebotomist was an unfriendly lady. I greeted her with a hearty "Good morning!" and she didn't even crack a smile. "What arm do you want it in?" she asked.

I decided to be friendly anyway. Maybe the woman who'd had her blood drawn before me was a pain in the butt. So I kept talking to the phlebotomist about this and that, "chatting her up," as the expression goes, but I didn't get much of a reaction out of her. Just as I was deciding that she was a person who didn't like to connect with strangers, she lightened up and began to tell me about her granddaughter.

Who knows why she wasn't the friendliest initially? Maybe she just gets started slowly. The main thing is that we connected and I lifted her spirits. She lifted my spirits too, because I was happy that I was able to make her happy.

Just then a woman with reddish gold hair came in and sat down to wait her turn. I thanked the phlebotomist on my way out the door. The two of us had made a connection, no matter how brief, and experienced all the benefits that came with our "micro-moment of shared positive emotion." And after all, you may as well make the best of having your blood drawn.

Paid to Play with Dogs

While waiting outside the Greater Cincinnati Memorial Day Dog Show barn, I saw the Golden Retrievers and Bernese Mountain Dogs make their way to the show ring. Their coats were perfectly combed and they walked in knowing they would be the center of attention, but I knew it had taken a lot of work by their handlers to make them that way.

I noticed a tall, beautiful young woman with fair skin and a smidgeon of freckles on her nose and cheeks. Her hair was pulled back in a bun and she was holding a Bernese Mountain Dog puppy.

"What a cute puppy!" I said.

"You can pet him if you want," she said, smiling. "His name is Klondike."

I gave him a good petting as she held him and he wiggled around and licked my wrist. "How old are you, Klondike?" I asked him.

"He's just four months old," the young woman answered.

I watched as some of Klondike's relatives made their way to the show ring. "So you're a handler?" I asked.

"Yes," she said with confidence. "I travel to shows every weekend. I'm from Indiana."

Another handler, a woman with long, gray, stringy hair parted in the middle, walked up to Klondike and gave him a kiss. Both the women laughed and then the grey-haired one said she had to go get Gracie and she'd be back.

"When I was a little girl," the handler from Indiana continued, "I didn't play with dolls; I played with stuffed animals and put dog leashes on all of them. I guess that pointed to my future as a dog handler." She paused. "I love what I do and wouldn't want to do anything else."

I admired her. Sometimes you meet someone who is so at home with who they are, that wherever they are, they are home. I had wondered about this subculture of dog handlers, groomers, breeders and vendors as I walked through rows and rows of RV's set up with tables outside and dogs playing behind octagonal fences. As I saw people sitting in small groups at tables with little shade, I remember thinking that you'd have to love this life to do this, because you travel every weekend. But there is always the element of adventure, and that in itself could keep you on an adrenaline high.

We would have gone on talking, but just then another handler waved to her to come help her. "Nice meeting you," she said. "Enjoy the show."

Remember, the Clerk Rules the Roost

Last night, for the first time, I tipped a clerk at the front desk of a hotel.

I was going to be booted out in the morning because the hotel was all booked up. I needed to stay an extra day, but there were no rooms available. So I went on the Internet in search of some assistance and support. I typed in "how to get a room in a fully booked hotel" and learned that if you find a helpful clerk, it's important to show your appreciation with a tip. I had no idea! Now I know and I like being in the know.

Wouldn't it be great not to have to schlep my stuff twenty minutes down the road to the next look-alike hotel? Armed with this new information, I marched to the front desk and politely asked the young male clerk with oversized glasses if any incoming guests had cancelled.

"No, not yet," he replied, without taking a look at the computer or at me. "Keep checking back."

Well, that wasn't what I call helpful. The hotel was clearly packed, but aren't these front desk people supposed to be clued-up or clued-in? My tip stayed in my pocket.

That evening, the clerk with the oversized glasses had been replaced by a friendly young woman with hipster black-rimmed glasses. Up to the front desk I went, pasting on my best confident smile. "Did any rooms open up for tomorrow night?" I asked her. "I've been hoping and hoping."

"No," she said, smiling, and reached for what appeared to be a hotel register. "What's your room number and name? I'll write it down."

Bingo! I knew that I had made a connection. She actually cared and had taken down my information, so I could put my new Internet tipping training to the test. The article said to give between five and twenty bucks. This wasn't New York City, so I handed over a nicely folded ten. She took it happily.

All these years, I had known about tipping the bellhops, the housekeepers, and the valets when I stayed at a hotel, but this new trick of tipping at the front desk had me returning to my room hopeful.

The next morning when I woke up, I turned over, crossed my fingers, and pressed the button for the front desk.

"Good morning," said a chipper voice I recognized. "May I help you?"

When I asked if a room had opened up, the helpful clerk replied quickly with enthusiasm, "Yes, we have a room for you and you don't even have to move. Just come down when you get a moment to get re-keyed."

"Hallelujah, hallelujah! Figaro!" I sang as I jumped out of bed.

Minutes later, leisurely sitting in the lobby drinking my coffee, I thought, Wow, this is so much better than packing up the toothpaste, fumbling for a lost shoe, and forgetting my phone charger. That was definitely the best ten bucks I had spent in a long time.

The Manicurist Who Never Did Her Homework

The manicurist I went to today was about twenty years old. She had long brown hair and was heavyset. I don't remember how we got on the subject of homework, but it's an interesting topic to me, because I think that most high school and junior high school students have too much homework these days. I'd rather see them having more time to try out new activities, develop their talents and hang out with their friends.

"Did you have a lot of homework when you were in high school?" I asked as she brushed a shiny pink coat of polish over my nails.

"I wouldn't know, because I never did any of it," she said.

Her answer startled me. If I were your mother, I thought, you would have done your homework. That's how you get into a good college.

But I said nothing. And then I started thinking. Would going to college have been the best thing for this young woman who chose to never do her homework?

In Robert Klose's book *The Three-Legged Woman and Other Excursions in Teaching,* he says, "Somewhere along the line during my college teaching career, an assumption (or directive) arose in American society that everyone should—must—go to college. The results have been in a word, mixed." He tells the story of one of his students named Brian who one day gave him a piece of cake that was so delicious that he said to him, "Go to cooking school."

We have this idea in America that everyone should want to go to college and become a professional. The truth of the matter is that not everyone does. And not everyone should. Isn't it ok for this young woman to choose to be a manicurist? She seems happy doing what she's doing.

Strangers with Word Limits

There's an increase in strangers with word limits who work in customer service departments. You've met them. Their jobs are in customer service, but they're not the least bit interested in customers.

You've been through the drill with them. They've cashed you out in the checkout line without exchanging a word or displaying an expression. They're paid to exchange some kind words, like "have a good day," but they don't. Why? Because no one is watching them.

The other day I met one of these types. He wasn't the worst I've ever come across in the "Word Limit Spectrum Disorder," but he was definitely in the category. I entered a lamp store and heard a man say, "You can put the lamp there." I was relieved that someone told me where to put the lamp, so I thought we were off to a good start, but I soon realized that these six words maxed out this gentleman's word limit. "You can put the lamp there" was all he had to say.

I watched him as he wound up my lamp cord. It was clear that, for him, the lamp cord had to be perfectly wound or nothing else would happen. So I waited patiently. I could have sworn I heard the ticking of a clock. Then there was a pause that seemed to turn into an eternity. He looked at my lamp and I looked at him. Finally, I asked, "What do we do next?"

"Well," he said slowly, "you want a lamp shade? Right?"

"Yes," I said and before I could say anything else, he

113

disappeared into a back room.

A few minutes later, he came out with a shade so close
to the one I had, it was almost uncanny. He took the
old shade off my lamp and put the new one on without
a word. He took the charge card that I held out to him
without a word. He handed me a receipt without a word.
I was wishing that the song "Happy" by Pharrell Williams
would suddenly start playing full blast in the background,
but it didn't.

I picked up my lamp. The new lampshade was wrapped
in a swirl of protective cellophane. I carried it down the
hall and opened the door carefully, balancing the lamp
so I didn't smash the new shade. I heard the sound of the
plastic wrapping on the shade crunch as it brushed across
my shoulder.

The man of few words could have:
  a. asked "Can I carry it for you?"
  b. said "Thank you for coming."
  c. said "Have a nice day."
  d. all of the above.

He did none of these things. Good thing, I thought, that I
don't buy lamp shades too often.

Boy, did he miss out, I thought. This man's self-imposed
word limit cut off all possibilities and opportunities for
connecting with new people. Boy, does he miss out—every
single day.

The Sunnyside Up Waitress

"Hey," the waitress said, smiling at me. I had barely walked in the door. She looked around the restaurant, as if she had just noticed that it was pretty empty. "I guess you can sit anywhere."

It was 2:45 p.m. The thing that's great about Waffle House is that even when you go at an odd time, it's not odd. There's always someone there or someone about to come in. If you want to talk, you can sit at the counter and strike up a conversation.

"So, do you know what you want or do you need a little time? Do you want some juice or coffee?" the waitress asked.

She had a sunny disposition. Her freckles seemed to match her friendly demeanor. She had fine straight brown hair to the top of her shoulders and warm delicate light brown eyes. I guessed her to be about nineteen.

We started talking because she wasn't busy. "I'm glad it's slow now," she said, "because it gives me a chance to think about this paper I have to write for my English class. You know, I'm taking four classes and it's all good because I work here in the morning five days a week and then I have three hours off in the afternoon before my classes. Two of my classes are online, which is great, and two are on campus. It's a good balance. It all works out because I get to see my fiancé in the late afternoon before my classes."

"Sounds like a good plan," I said.

I was thinking that someone else might complain about having to work five days a week and take four classes and try to save some money for a wedding and college, but instead she was grateful.

What is happiness? This is something I've been pondering lately. Why is it that some people waste their time complaining and holding grudges while other people just make the best of what's handed to them?

A man with a cane got up slowly from a booth. "Bye," he said to the waitress.

"I'll get the door for you," she said and ran around the counter to help him.

"I'm fine, I can get it…"

"No, it's okay," she said and held it open. "Bye, have a good day, see you soon."

"Is he a regular?" I asked her.

"Yes, he comes in here a couple times a week. He's so cute."

"You know," she said, turning to the manager, who had just walked in from the back room, "Jack didn't come in today. I hope he's okay. Maybe I should call him. Maybe he's sick."

"He'll be fine," the manager said. "Let's worry about it if he doesn't show up tomorrow."

I was amazed that they kept the phone numbers of their

regulars, or at least some of them. How touching that they keep an eye out for them.

I looked at the waitress. She was talking to a truck driver in the corner booth. She poured him a coffee. They said something to each other. She laughed and then he laughed.

She'll do just fine in life, I thought. It's such a pleasure for everyone to spend time with someone who has a sunny disposition.

The Most Charming Pizza Delivery Man on Earth

Have you ever had a memorable pizza delivery man?

The last time I ordered a pizza, I got a call about 45 minutes later. The delivery man said he was a couple of blocks away from my house and wanted to make sure he knew where I lived. While I was explaining the directions to him, the phone went silent. I wasn't sure if he was on the line or if the call got dropped. Then he said, "I'm so sorry, but I just saw the most beautiful thing, I just saw like ten deer."

"Wow! that's great," I said. "We have a lot of deer back here."

"But I've never been where you live. It's so beautiful."

His words gave me pause. "Well, the deer are beautiful, but you have to be careful driving."

"They were just so amazing!" He was almost breathless. "I'll be there in a moment," he added, as if we were old friends.

What a grateful person, I thought, to take so much pleasure in seeing deer.

Before I saw his car pull up, I already liked him. And he already liked me. So when I opened the front door, we stood there for just a moment, smiling at each other.

He was all of nineteen or twenty, with short-cropped blond hair and a kind face. He was past the age of innocence, but seemingly still innocent.

"There was a deer right there, too." He pointed at the living room window.

"They do come right up to our house sometimes," I said. "Sometimes in the morning, I open a shade and there's a deer right there."

I couldn't keep from smiling at him. "I hope you see some more deer," I said. I thanked him for the pizza and gave him a big tip.

Later that night, after dinner, dishes and laundry, I picked up my phone. There was a text that said, "You are one of the most beautiful and nicest people I've ever had the honor of delivering a pizza to. Thank you very much. I hope nothing bad ever happens to you."

I smiled to myself, delighted. I had never gotten a text like that before. Some people keep their sense of wonder to themselves. He was so willing to share his appreciation, and it was contagious.

STRANGERS IN CLOSE QUARTERS

Here's Where You Get Off

One minute my daughter Olivia and I are driving home from Nashville, somewhere outside of Louisville, pretty much in the middle of nowhere on I-71. The next minute we're stopped on the roadside because my car was signaling "low engine pressure" as we drove down a winding hill.

The auto club sent a tow truck driven by a very big man with short-cropped red hair, huge arms, and muscular shoulders. Let's put it this way, he was not a person I would want to meet in a dark alley. The idea of sitting next to him on a truck seat all the way back to Cincinnati could be intimidating, but since Olivia and I both like talking with people we don't know, we were okay with it.

We were standing outside while he eased my car onto his tow truck. It was cold and dark. The wind was whipping around empty Styrofoam cups by the gas pumps.

"You can get in," he said. "It's warm in the truck."

"Thanks!" We somehow hoisted ourselves in. I was in the middle with the stick shift between my legs, but I was happy. The truck was warm; thank goodness we were headed back home on this cold night.

Once we began driving, I decided to start chatting—break the ice, as they say. "Did you ever drive someone for a couple of hours who never said a word the whole way?"

"Ah, sure, I have people that are up against the door."

Olivia and I laughed at that image. How was leaning against the door going 75 miles an hour going to help them?

The three of us talked on and off for a while, and then there was a pause that went on for miles. "Did you ever have people that are nuts?" I finally asked.

He got quiet for a minute. "Sure I have. A few weeks ago, I picked up a drunk guy and his girlfriend. He started cussing at her and she took a swing at him. It missed the boyfriend and hit me in the eye. I said to them, 'Here's where you get off,' and I left him and his girlfriend on the highway."

When I heard this story, at first I felt sorry for the two of them being left on the highway, and then I didn't feel sorry for them at all. I was proud of the driver for dumping them off. He doesn't deserve to be hit in the eye. Who knows what could have happened to him next?

"That's why I always carry a gun," he said. "You have to have a gun 'cause you never know."

I found myself wondering where he stored it.

"I work hard," he said. "I take the shifts that no one wants, the ones where you have to drive people far out of town." He added, "I don't like Cincinnati much. I was mugged there. This guy walked up to me and held a gun to my head and then I saw there were two men behind him."

I looked at Olivia and she looked at me.

"Mind if I smoke?" he asked.

"Yes, I do," I said, "but if you want to stop somewhere that's fine."

"It's going to be a long ride," he said.

Then I got a bit worried. I didn't think he'd drop us off on the highway, but it's one of those developments in a relationship where you hit your first bump in the road and you're not sure where it's headed.

After that, the truck went silent except for the radio playing Brad Paisley's song "She's Everything."

Right before it got too awkward and we became the passengers up against the door, he said, "Did you ever eat at Penn Station? I like that place a lot."

"It's really good," I said.

"I love the chicken teriyaki!" Olivia said.

"I love the fries," I added.

"I think I'm going to get me some of those on my way home," he said.

We turned down the road towards the auto dealer who was going to fix my car, and there was a Penn Station lit up in a nearby strip mall.

"There's a Penn Station," I said, pointing.

"That's great," he said.

He pulled up to the auto dealer. My daughter and I

climbed out of the truck. I gave him a tip and thanked him for taking us all the way there.

My friend Mike was waiting in his car to take us home. As we drove away, Olivia and I looked over at Penn Station and saw the tow truck parked a half a block back in the empty lot.

I pictured him enjoying his French fries, all the while knowing when he was done that he'd have to backtrack down the same path that got him there.

Hopefully, there'd be no more calls for his services tonight. No more calls that could possibly shift from an ordinary tow to his telling someone to get out of his truck. Or worse, drawing his gun because someone went one step too far.

The Thoughts of a Stranger Running Out of Time

Ace Hardware, 10:05 a.m., Monday. I'm standing in line to pay for my floodlights. A silver-haired lady in her eighties with a faint black line of a mustache and pale translucent skin gets behind me.

"What a big line," she says to me, "this early in the morning."

"I know," I say.

"It's going to be very hot today," she says and shakes her head.

"It sure is."

"I'm a Depression-era baby." She looks right into my eyes. "I've seen how bad it can get."

As she speaks, the man in a torn brown t-shirt in front of me moves up in line. "This weather, and the economy, and the wildfires in Colorado, it makes you think that the world is going to end, doesn't it?"

I nod in agreement even though I don't agree. I think there are times when it's best to just agree with someone as long as it does no harm. Agreeing with her isn't going to cost me anything. I'm not in my eighties; I haven't lived through the Depression.

She notices that I am next in line and she has only seconds

left to tell me her thoughts, the thoughts of a stranger running out of time. "Look at what's going on in Europe," she says. "It's just falling apart."

I put my three floodlights on the counter as I nod at her. "You're right, Europe is not doing well."

The cashier frowns at us. She just wants me to cash out, not talk. But I turn back anyway to speak a few more words to this silver-haired stranger holding her bottle of Windex. "Have a good day," I say, wishing I could wipe away the worry in her eyes.

Mr. Flirt

As the airplane doors were closing, I was thrilled that no one was sitting in the middle seat next to me. I wanted to shout, Yes! Yes! Yes!

It never happens anymore and yet, there it was—a wide, empty space between me and the young, heavyset woman in the window seat. "Can you believe it?" I said.

"Yeah, right!" she said. Not the language that I would have used, but nevertheless a response.

I could stretch out, put my pile of books and magazines in the middle and throw my leg over as far as I wanted! As my elation escalated a man suddenly appeared from the back of the plane and practically jumped over me into the middle seat. No way! I thought.

As he squeezed past me, he said, "I just gave my seat to a guy so he could sit next to his girlfriend."

"That's nice," I said, gritting my teeth.

Then he turned to his left and said to the window seat woman, "Are you afraid to fly? I can hold your hand." She laughed and laughed. Well, he was young and good-looking. And she was clearly enjoying his attention.

"No, I mean it," he said. She laughed and pulled her red Delta loaner blanket tighter around her very large chest.

He then turned back to me. "What part of flying do you like best?"

"Landing," I said very matter-of-factly.

"That's very funny," he said, smiling at me. He paused like he was going to file that line in his brain somewhere to use in a similar situation.

He talked to the red blanket woman a little more. He practically whispered in her ear. It was a bit too close for strangers, but she seemed comfortable.

Later, when we hit some turbulence, he asked her again if she wanted to hold his hand. She laughed it off and leaned against the seat, trying not to look nervous, even though I could tell she was not a good flyer.

I'll give her credit for handling Mr. Flirt so well. There's a lot to be said for managing all kinds of people, but I think she knew he was harmless. And I think he made her feel good about herself.

He saw me writing a note in my book and asked if I had a pen he could borrow. I lent him my least favorite, thinking that I probably wouldn't get it back. Along with the pen, I gave him a peppermint candy. I thought it might calm him down. He was a bit hyperactive, between his iPhone poker games, a book he pretended to read whose cover I never saw and his third cup of coffee. He fidgeted a lot and leaned over his knapsack looking for things and shuffling items around.

To my surprise, when we landed he handed me my pen back.

Upon disembarking he said to the skycap waiting with a wheelchair, "Is that for me?"

129

"Not yet," the guy said. And the two of them laughed.

I decided I liked him. He might have been too flirty, but he was a person who appreciated laughter, created laughter and could find laughter in seconds. He brought out the best in people and that was a gift. And he was willing to make a trade so a couple could sit together. Okay, maybe it wasn't so bad that I didn't have that extra space on my flight home.

The Empty Seat Next to You

One of the most common locations for finding a stranger is in the seat next to you. It's the seat that was unoccupied a few minutes ago, but now holds someone you don't know, someone you've never seen. This person could possibly change the entire course of your life, or just make for an enjoyable evening—or perhaps a nerve-racking one.

Tonight my daughter Olivia and I are the strangers ready to find good empty seats at the open-air amphitheater at Chautauqua Institution, a mecca of cultural and educational opportunities in Chautauqua, New York. We're looking for not only the right viewing location for the Jennifer Nettles concert we're attending, but also neighbors we can live with for a while.

The seats are first-come, first-served benches (think church pews). I know from experience that at a popular event like this, we'll most likely be squeezed next to whomever is seated next to us.

I spot a young woman who's what I'd call a "cool-looking person" seated next to a guy that looks friendly and "cool" as well. She has hip green glasses, lots of stylish jewelry and a friendly smile. "Are these seats free?" I ask.

"Yes," she says cheerfully as the two of them scoot over. Maybe she's relieved that friendly-looking people like us will be their seat-mates. I ask her if she's seen Jennifer Nettles before. She says she has, and adds, "She's great!" Then she tells Olivia that she likes her bracelet. After Olivia thanks her, she says, "Don't just think it, it's good to say something nice to someone if that's what you're thinking.

131

That's what I believe."

I like her philosophy. I tell her that my daughter, who goes by the stage name Olivia Frances (www. oliviafrancesmusic.com), is a musician and song-writer. And then I pause.

"You should brag on her," she says.

I take my iPhone out and press iTunes to show the two of them a song from Olivia's album, "Back to Happiness." She holds the phone up to her ear and her friend leans in close.

They smile and listen to the whole song, which I didn't expect them to do—but I love them for it.

When the music starts she and Olivia begin dancing in their seats, waving their arms back and forth in sync with each other. It's beautiful to watch, like two old friends who have practiced these dance moves many times before. The "cool" guy and I sit on either side of them clapping along with the audience in rhythm.

When it's time to go, we finally introduce ourselves to each other. I tell Dawn and Todd how nice it was to meet them.

"Good luck with your music, Olivia," Dawn says, and there are smiles all around from the four of us. A concert is so much more enjoyable when you share the music and a bench with people whose company you enjoy—like these people in the seats next to us to whom we were strangers just a few short hours ago.

Her Kitchen Story

The waitress took my order without much interest. It was pushing 2:30 p.m. and I was one of her few customers. After she brought me an iced tea, she went back into the kitchen and I heard her on the phone clear as day.

"Can't you just bring me my medicine?" Pause. "What?" Pause. "You're such an asshole. I've been working since 6:00 a.m. I don't feel well. You can get off the couch and bring me my medicine. You're a shit." Pause. "What?" Pause. "A real shit."

That was the end of the conversation. She didn't slam the handset down because she didn't have one to slam. All the drama and power encompassed in a landline phone had been reduced to a silent tap on a pathetic cellphone.

In the delay that followed, I imagined her trying to calm down before she came out of the kitchen. When she did, she went up to one of her customers—a heavy-set man with a pink face—and stood stiffly as she set down his order of toast and poured him some searing hot coffee. He didn't say a word.

I acted like I hadn't heard her one-way conversation, staring into my phone as if something riveting was happening there. All three of us customers were trying to pretend her words away, as if we could go back before the toast popped.

Why do we do that? Why do we pretend not to hear? Human nature, I guess. She had needed to make a phone call, but the only place she could make it while working

was within our earshot. So we were all part of her story.
We didn't know whom she had talked to, but it sounded
bad. Real bad. I felt badly for her.

She turned and went back into the kitchen and came out
with my turkey sandwich. She put it down a bit more
loudly than necessary. "Anything else I can get you?" she
asked. Her face flushed with anger, not tears.

"No, I'm good."

When I went to pay, she took my twenty-dollar bill and
gave me back my change slowly, as if she was thinking
about something.

"Thanks," I said.

Then, as I stepped away from the cash register, she said,
"My husband is such an asshole. I work two jobs. He
works one. We're living in a hotel while we try to get our
lives in order. I take care of the kids. He doesn't help. He
can't even bring me my medicine. When I serve him with
divorce papers, he better not act surprised."

"I'm sorry you work two jobs and he works one," I said.

"Yeah, he's so lazy. So lazy! I can't even stand it."

I saw the short order cook look over at her as he scraped at
the grill. I could tell he had heard about her sorry husband
plenty of times before and he was going to keep hearing
about him, whether he wanted to or not. He looked at
me, but not with an I-feel-sorry-for-you,-customer,-that-
you-had-to-listen-to-her-story kind of look. No, he just
looked at me as if to say, Isn't this the way everyone lives,

listening to each other's kitchen stories?

Somehow her scenario struck me as a universal one: the lazy husband, the unhappy wife who pulls all the weight. The home that isn't really a home and the children stuck in the middle of all the unhappiness. It was a story I heard plenty of times while teaching my community college writing classes, from some of my older female college students who had families. (Only without the swear words. After all, they were writing for a grade.)

All I could hope for this waitress was for her to have a little privacy and the strength to change her story so she wouldn't have to tell this one to strangers again and again.

Soldier on Board

"Hi, I've got the window seat," I said to the man in the aisle seat, who looked like a teddy bear.

"Oh, sure," he said and jumped up a little too quickly, bumping his head on the ceiling of the small plane.

"Are you okay?" I asked.

He nodded and gave me room to slip into my seat.

"Well," he said, as he snapped his seatbelt closed. "All we can do is make the best of it."

"Yes," I said. I noticed that his upper left arm was touching mine. There was nothing he could do. He was a big guy and there just wasn't enough room for his body.

"I'm going to my cousin's wedding," I said.

"That's great," he said. "I'm headed home. I'm going home after seven weeks for treatment for PTSD."

I paused for a minute, not knowing what to say.

I settled on, "Wow. How are you feeling?"

"I'm doing better."

Here I had thought I was sitting next to a young man with his future ahead of him. Instead I was sitting next to a young man who was fighting to get his future back. And he had done all this for our country. I felt honored to sit next to him.

"Did you know," he said, "that the Cincinnati area has one of the best PTSD clinics in the country? It's actually in Fort Mitchell, Kentucky."

"No," I said, "I didn't know that." I wanted to ask him so many questions, but I decided I shouldn't because it could trigger bad memories for him.

"I hope we get there soon," he said, looking a bit nervous as he turned to me. "What is it, an hour or so flight?"

"I think that's about right."

"I have my medicine," he said and tapped at the front left pocket of his fatigues.

I was wondering if he was going to need my help on the flight. Would loud noises startle him?

"Do you have any family in the military?" I asked.

"My dad was in Vietnam. I can't imagine what he went through."

When the flight attendant came by to take our drink order, he asked for apple juice, took a few sips, then opened his medicine bottle and popped a pill into his mouth. He looked relieved after he took it.

While I read a book, I saw him trying to rest his eyes, but it didn't work.

"I got another flight after this," he said.

"That's too bad," I said. "But you'll be home soon."

After we landed and he was standing in the aisle about to depart the plane, I said, "It was nice talking with you."

I thought he was going to shake my hand, but instead he held the palm of his hand out to me. I pressed my hand against his. It was the warmest, most inviting hand I had touched in a long time.

Friends in a Jiffy

Recently, I went to a Jiffy Lube for an oil change. I got there early in the morning expecting an empty waiting room and then saw I was not the first to arrive. There was a tall, thin black man in his thirties already seated, looking intently at his cell phone.

"Hi," I said to him.

"Hi," he said back. I could tell he was surprised I'd spoken.

I sat down and started scrolling on my iPhone. "Have you found any promo codes for Jiffy Lube coupons?" I asked.

"No," he said. "You can do that? I didn't know that."

"Yeah," I said. "A friend of mine told me about promo coupons and everywhere I go now, I check. I've found a lot. But sometimes they're expired."

I saw him scrolling through his phone.

"Wait a minute," he said, "I see a ten-dollar one. Oops, it's expired. Here's a five-dollar one." He smiled and held up his phone for me to see.

A few minutes later, a mechanic called him up to the counter. After he paid using his coupon, he turned to me and said, "Hey, thanks."

"You're welcome," I said.

I knew we both felt better for having talked to each

other—and that saving $5 was a very small part of it. We could have sat in that room with that awkward silence of two humans stuck in a space saying nothing. Instead, we forged a small connection that left us both smiling.

STRANGERS WITH CHUTZPAH

Never Meddle with a Locksmith

When a locksmith came on Monday morning to fix a lock that was sticking, I was hoping he wasn't creepy—after all, he does have the ability to access my house.

I didn't need to have worried. I could sense the kindness in his heart from the minute I opened the door. He was a big burly man with a wide grin and wrinkles by the corners of his blue eyes. I looked at his face and sensed he had lived a life that had been hard in some ways but was satisfying nonetheless.

The first thing he did was bend down on his knees to pet my dog, Trixie. The two of them nuzzled and fussed like they were old friends.

"You have dogs, don't you?" I asked him.

"I've got three rescues," he said, and went on to tell me about each of them. I was glad he liked to talk. I figured, given the work he does, he would have a lot of interesting stories. I'm sure people lock themselves into and out of some real predicaments. I thought he might tell me about a few.

And sure enough, when we walked passed the powder room, he had a story for me. But it wasn't about one of his customers. Instead he said, "I put an alarm on my medicine cabinet because of my snoopy sister-in-law."

"You what?" I said. "Your sister-in-law takes things from your medicine cabinet?"

"No, she doesn't take things, she just snoops. Anyway, on Thanksgiving last year I rigged the medicine cabinet. During dinner she excused herself and I told the family that the medicine cabinet alarm was going to go off in 10, 9, 8... Sure enough it went off. It was painfully loud and she came back to the table beet red. Boy, was she embarrassed."

"Well," I said, "I guess she won't do that again."

"Nope, that took care of it."

I admired his principles. He truly valued privacy. This was a man who not only rescued dogs, but, if pushed, would use his skills to put a person who was out of line in their place. Never meddle with a locksmith, I thought.

One More Way to Use a Cultivator

We had just finished a barbecue dinner and were hanging out on my friend Kim's deck, admiring her beautiful zinnias.

"Did I ever tell you," she asked, as she started to clear the dishes, "the story about my Uncle Nate's gardener?"

We all shook our heads.

"Uncle Nate had a man, Pete, who worked for him for many years, doing odd jobs and taking care of the yard. My uncle traveled for work and wasn't home much." She paused. "One day, my uncle went down to the basement looking for something. He opened the door to a room and to his complete surprise he saw a man in there. It was Pete the gardener sprawled out on the couch, drinking a can of beer and watching the Chicago Cubs. 'What are you doing here?' my uncle demanded. 'How did you get in here?'

"You'd have to know my eccentric uncle," Kim said. "He was surprised, not scared, to find Pete and he wanted some answers.

"'I needed a place to stay,' Pete told him. 'Sorry about that. I just used my cultivator to get the window open and came in. I've been here for a few days.'

"I can just picture Uncle Nate taking a few puffs from his cigar as Pete gathered up his things," Kim said.

By now we were all laughing at the thought that someone could be living in your house without your even knowing it. I think every one of us checked our basements that night.

Near Naked Yoga

A friend of mine told me about a friend of hers who tried out a new class this week at the yoga studio she regularly attends.

The male teacher, a stranger to her, had undressed slowly during the class, stripping off various layers of clothing, and by the end he was only wearing a jock strap.

Her friend was very uncomfortable witnessing this man shed his decency one piece at a time. She wondered how he could think his behavior was acceptable, and she was stunned by the boldness of it. How come he didn't know what his boundaries were?

I wondered what made this yoga guy think that showing off his buttocks in a million different poses was okay with his students. Why didn't he just call his class "Near Naked Yoga?" To me the whole thing smacks of a man out of control, flaunting his body when no one asked for his body to be flaunted.

This flasher/teacher moment sounds like an episode from Larry David's *Curb Your Enthusiasm*. I can just picture the students catching each other's eyes and grimacing, but not saying anything until afterward, when they commiserated with one another in the parking lot.

Some people will really act out if they have an audience—and an unsuspecting, captive one was perfect for this man's agenda.

Sounds like this man/boy needs to turn his focus from

Yoga to Life Modelling. At least when the class arrives they'll know what they came for and why they paid to look at him.

The iPad Snooper

I was reading on my iPad sitting in the baggage claim section of United Airlines when a stranger's shadow crossed over me. I felt like maybe I should scream. This person was way too close. He was definitely invading my personal space.

Baggage claim was so quiet. Why was this person so close?

Then I heard a voice. "Don't you love those iPads? You can just read them anywhere. I keep mine in the car all the time."

I looked up at a slick-haired man with a dark tan and very white teeth. He was so excited about this technology that he stopped in his tracks to discuss it with me, a stranger in the middle of reading a book. Jeffrey Englander's *What We Talk about When We Talk about Anne Frank*, to be specific.

"Yeah, they're great." That's what I said. But when I think about it, I have mixed feelings about my iPad. I'm happy to have instant access to thousands of books, but unhappy I can't physically riffle through its pages or doodle in it.

I had mixed feelings about this slick-haired man, too. Much as I love talking with strangers, when I'm in the middle of a good story I don't want to be interrupted. If I'd had my nose buried in a book instead of an iPad, chances are he would have walked on by and left my personal space, well, personal.

It seems my iPad made me appear as instantly accessible as the books it makes available to me. That's technology for you—sometimes all that instant accessibility is overwhelming.

Of Course You Will

I turned at the bend in the road and saw a tall, gangly man jogging towards me in the distance. I didn't recognize him and before I could say "one potato, two potato," he ran rapidly towards me and then stopped next to me and I mean NEXT TO ME. Who does that? I thought. This is one of the brashest people I've ever encountered and I don't like it one bit.

"Can I use your phone?" he asked me, while sweat poured down his silvered sideburns. He wasn't the least bit panicked about anything. He was as cool as a cucumber, but he wanted my phone. How did I know he wasn't going to take off with it? I felt like saying, "A friendly 'hello' would have started us off on a better track."

"AND WHO ARE YOU?" I asked him boldly, hoping to startle him. It worked. He looked a bit taken aback. He told me his name, which is an unusual one. It turns out I know his brother. He didn't ask me my name and I didn't offer it. This encounter was all about the phone. And clearly, because he didn't attempt an introduction, this was a man who was used to getting what he wanted.

"Okay," I said, "since I know your brother, I'll let you use my phone." The fear that he might steal my new iPhone 6 and run had subsided.

"I need to call my wife," he said. "The battery on my phone is dead."

Then I handed it over to him. Still angry, still wondering why I had lent it to him. Was it because I was a woman that he thought he'd have a good chance of me saying yes to him? If I was a big scary-looking man, would he have asked to borrow it? I think not. At that moment I wanted to be a big scary man and frighten him away, but instead I heard him leave a message for his wife.

"Hi, Lauren," he said. "I just wanted you to know that my cell phone is dead. I'll be back in a few minutes."

"Thanks," he said, handing me back my now-sweat-covered phone and jogging away. I shook my head in disbelief.

Well, at least he said thanks, I thought as I watched him run down the road. If he ever asks me again, the answer is no, definitely no.

Pumping a Captive Audience

There are usually no surprises at the gas pump, except
for the price tag. But this time was different. I drove up,
stopped my car and was looking at my phone when all of a
sudden, I noticed a man was standing too close to my open
car window, displaying a product in a can.

"Would you like to try this product?" he asked. He was a
young, sandy-haired man, with a sweaty forehead. "This
will shine up your tires. It's unbelievable how good they'll
look…"

"No, thank you," I said to him. Annoyed.

"Well, let me just show you…" he said in a hyper, pushy
way, holding the can even closer for me to see.

I looked him right in the eye. "No means no," I said and
paused.

I was lovin' the long pause. I didn't utter another word. He
was surprised, like he'd been rejected before, but not quite
this way, and he just stood there for a moment processing
it before he turned away.

Well, I thought to myself. He's got a tough job; it's a job
full of rejection day after day. I wonder what his daily sales
quota is, but I'm not going to help him reach it.

A silver Toyota Camry pulled up at the pump across from
me and I saw him run over to it.

A woman in her thirties with Farrah Fawcett hair climbed

out. He began explaining the tire product to her. I heard her giggle—that's right, giggle—and then I saw her flirting with him. "You can try it on my tires," I heard her say. She twirled a strand of her hair and watched him spray her tires.

Different strokes for different folks, I thought. Maybe his sales quota will be just fine today.

STRANGERS IN DIFFERENT CIRCLES

Thirty Thousand Strangers under the Age of Thirty

I spent last week with 30,000 strangers under the age of thirty at the South by Southwest Music Festival (SXSW) in Austin, Texas. The hip event drew music- and film-lovers from all over the world. I heard many languages spoken—the ones I could identify were Spanish, Dutch, German and French.

My daughter, Olivia, a seventeen-year-old singer song-writer, attended SXSW because she was selected to be one of the performers at a venue run by GoGirls Music, a community organization that promotes, supports and empowers indie women musicians.

Of course, I had to see her perform, and so did her Nana, who flew in, too. Olivia had a general admission ticket so she wouldn't miss a thing. My mom and I did not, because the tickets were expensive and we weren't planning to go to many shows. We used most of our time in Austin for sightseeing and people-watching. The result was that we felt really old!

After Olivia's performance, the two of us tag-alongs did some serious SXSW people watching, which made us feel really old. E-cigarettes everywhere, tattoos galore in some painful parts of the body (just in case you didn't know, big trend: necklace design tattoos on women; when I look at them, I think "ouch, my décolletage"), and sightings of numerous ear gauges on men that I just don't get. Lots of drinking and drugs, of course—this is a music festival. Ambulance sirens blasting continually, unnerving my mom and me. Everywhere we went, we heard people talking about their hangovers. Not to mention the hotel shuttle we couldn't take one night because the driver warned us that someone had just thrown up in it. My biggest worry: the stoned people that ambled straight across streets, oblivious to traffic coming right at them.

If I felt outdated, my mom must have thought she was part of a museum exhibit, but she handled it really well, moving slowly but with intention through the crowds. My favorite sighting was a man in his fifties with a t-shirt that said, "I'm not moving to Austin." I wanted to get a matching one.

There was no relief from the music, not even in our hotel room, where we heard a thumping raucous bass pounding away from early afternoon until the wee hours of the night. (Later, we discovered it was coming from a venue across the street.) I found it so irritating that I've never been so grateful for owning headphones—I put them on just to hear myself think. Music is a pleasure, but not at 1 a.m. night after night—and not ALL music.

Olivia, on the other hand, loved every minute of SXSW and used every second well. She sold CD's, handed out hundreds of business cards, and made some great contacts. She even met Suzanne Vega—and was thrilled that Suzanne started following her music.

Her Nana and I were so happy for her. We were also glad when it was all over and we didn't have to keep waiting for cabs for an hour or more anytime we wanted to go anywhere.

I was very tired when I returned to Cincinnati; so was my

mom when she went back to Florida. Am I glad I went? Yes. SXSW is not an everyday experience. And now, two days later, I'm just emerging from the overstimulation. But it was all worth it, and not just because I got to see my daughter perform. It's fascinating to be immersed in another generation's world.

Hey, What's That Monkey Doing on My Head?

Every once in a while you come across an old photo of yourself that at first seems so unfamiliar that you feel like a stranger to yourself. You find yourself asking, "Is that really me?" when in fact you know it is.

That's how I felt yesterday when my daughter Olivia found an old photo of me with a monkey on my head. I looked a bit squirmy, like I was wishing the moment was over. Well, it's not every day that there's a monkey on your head.

"Do you remember this photo?" she asked.

"I kind of do and I kind of don't," I told her. I stared at the picture. I think I'm about seventeen and I'm somewhere in Greece. I'd forgotten about the monkey, but now that I think about it, I remember him.

I didn't particularly like having him on my head. I was worried that he would poop on me and I didn't like his screeching. I was probably only with that little monkey for a minute or two, but that minute or two was enough for me.

While I squinted at the photo, I tried to remember who gave me the monkey to hold. Then, slowly, across a dusty part of my brain, a pathway cleared and a vague memory of a rotund, middle-aged man, a street vendor, appeared. "Do you want to hold my monkey?" he had asked me in a heavy accent.

"Yes, that's it!" I shouted, and I shared these details with Olivia, proud that I could reconstruct the scene all these years later.

The great thing about old photos is the ability to catch glimpses of your younger self. I like this glimpse because it is of me being bold. Today, I wouldn't hold that monkey for anything—been there, done that, as they say. There's a comfort and wisdom in being middle-aged, not needing to prove myself to a monkey, or anyone else for that matter. Let some other teen give that monkey a try…

Mission: Talk to Strangers

The other day, as my daughter was sitting on a bench catching some sun before her music lesson at the University of Cincinnati, two young women came up to her.

"Hi," one of them said, "what are you doing?" She wore a short-sleeved maroon t-shirt with a long, flowing floral skirt. Her friend was wearing a long skirt too.

"Studying French," Olivia answered as her mind raced. Do I know these women? I don't think so.

"What other classes do you take?" the floral-skirted woman asked. She was obviously the more talkative of the two.

"I don't go to school here," my daughter said. "I'm in high school. Do you go here?"

"No," the woman answered. "We're Mormons. We travel around the country talking to people."

It was then that my daughter realized that these women were trying to convert her. She took it in stride. The three of them talked a few more minutes about this and that. Somewhere in their brief conversation, they asked my daughter what religion she was and she told them that she was Jewish and was happy to be Jewish. After that the young women must have realized that it was time to move on. They said their goodbyes.

As they walked away toward a small group of students

sitting on the steps of a nearby building, my daughter thought about how many strangers they must talk to in a day. How often do they find a person interested in becoming a Mormon and how many times a day are they rebuked?, she wondered.

"The young women were very happy spending their days talking to people about their religion," she told me that night as we sat at our kitchen table having a cup of Earl Grey tea. "They told me that they had grown up Mormon and that they knew exactly how to live their lives because the Bible tells them all the answers."

Olivia was amazed by the women's strong beliefs. "'All the answers,'" she repeated. Wow." And then she took another sip of tea.

Breakfast with a Psychic Seeker

One minute I'm waiting for a table at a packed Waffle House. The next minute I'm seated in a booth across from a stranger, sharing breakfast with her.

Well, it didn't happen that quickly, but close. I had been waiting in line ahead of her and struck up a conversation. "Wow," I said, "I didn't think that it was going to be this crowded!"

She said, "Yeah, I'm surprised too. I'm going to the Psychic Festival, but I'd rather eat here. It's cheaper."

The Psychic Festival, I thought. I wonder why she's into that. Now, she's a person I'd like to talk to. A booth opened up and the host told me a table was available. "Want to join me?" I asked.

"Sure," she said. "I hate to take up a booth when I'm by myself."

We sat down and had that awkward moment of not knowing what to say to each other. Curiously, the two of us took our phones out of our purses at the exact same time and placed them on the table, like security blankets.

Just then, a worn-out-looking waitress with frizzy brown hair came over and said to my booth-mate, "How's it going, Tracy?"

"It's good, Mary Ann," she said. She nodded at me and added, "We just met." Then she turned back to Mary Ann. "I'm headed to the Psychic Festival after this."

163

"I'm real interested in that," Mary Ann said, "but I'm scared. I don't want to hear anything that I don't want to hear, but I believe in all that. I do. I really do."

"You should go," Tracy said.

Mary Ann went over to take an order from a man so big he took up almost two seats at the counter.

"I'm really into everything psychic," Tracy said to me. "You see, my dad died a month ago and I want to meet with a medium and talk to him. I took care of him when he was dying. I miss him and I want to talk with him."

Her eyes teared up and I felt badly for her. "I'm sorry about your dad," I said.

"Thanks, it's hard. It's really hard," she said. And then she went right back to talking about the Psychic Festival. "It costs forty dollars for a reading and twenty dollars to get in, but all the classes are free. I'm totally into it."

With her jet black hair in its severe Cleopatra cut and her supersized hoop earrings, she looked like someone who would hang out at a psychic festival.

"I've had readings done for years," she went on. "Sometimes they're dead-on and sometimes they aren't. Doesn't matter to me. I'm still going to go."

"I've never been to a psychic festival," I said.

"You should go," she said very matter-of-factly, just like she had to Mary Ann. "There's a medium that I want to meet with. For some reason, I'm drawn to her picture." She picked up her phone and showed me the face of a middle-aged woman with sandy blonde hair.

"I hope that she works out for you."

"Me too," she said. "I have a daughter who's seven. I don't take her to psychic festivals, I think it can be too weird for a kid. We watch psychics on TV though."

I thought it was pretty weird that she let her seven-year-old watch those shows, but I didn't say anything.

When our food arrived, Tracy got some sort of egg sandwich creation that I couldn't identify. Since she was a regular, Mary Ann had brought it out without even taking her order, but Lord knows what it was. It looked like a gloppy mess.

I wanted to stare at it, as if to figure out how I would describe it if I were a food writer. You know, as if I were writing one of those road food books. But I didn't, I asked her another question about the Psychic Festival, and she went on talking about it.

I was aware that Tracy hadn't asked me anything. She was either too grief-stricken or not interested or both. At one point I told her I was a writer and she didn't even ask me what I wrote. I didn't mind. Sometimes people just need to talk to someone they don't know.

When we were finished, she said, "Well, thanks for letting me share your booth."

"Anytime," I said.

We walked out together. Her dusty black Jeep was parked next to my car. She got into it and waved goodbye. I waved back, hoping that she would find what she was searching for.

Dasher, Dancer, Prancer and All Things Christmas

When I was a child, Christmas was a difficult and intriguing time. Since I'm Jewish and most of my friends were Christian, I was constantly reminded that I was different. Yes, I celebrated Hanukkah with my family and ate potato latkes and applesauce, but when it came right down to it, the traditions of Hanukkah couldn't compare to all things Christmas.

I remember wanting to sit on Santa's lap, gaze at his long white beard, tell him what I wanted for Christmas and have my picture taken with him. I imagined myself in a red velvet Christmas dress and a red bow, complete with a sprig of holly, in my hair. I pictured the wreath we would have on our front door, the smell of pine that welcomed everyone to our home.

The Christmas trees I saw tucked so carefully inside their netting on the rooftops of cars were so beautiful to me. I even loved the artificial silver trees that stood in the living rooms of some of my childhood friends. I longed for a Christmas tree of my own that you could see lit up through the front window of our house. It would have a silver star on top that just missed touching the ceiling, and there would be boxes and boxes of ornaments for me to hang.

I wanted to wrap presents in green-and-red gift paper with gold bows, not the blue-and-white Hanukkah paper of my faith. I itched to sing "White Christmas" loudly, like it was my holiday song. Instead I whisper-sang it when it played on the radio. Perhaps I thought it was a betrayal to be heard singing it.

Christmas cookies were almost too much for me: the boxes and trays of cutout snowmen and Santas, candy canes and stockings. I loved eating them and was amazed at how my friends were able to bake and decorate so many. The gingerbread man cookies were my favorite. I loved their three white frosted buttons, their cute smiles and their spicy scent.

Just once I wanted to see Santa and his reindeer flying through the sky. I wanted to wear a flashy red Christmas sweater and go ice-skating. Decorate our house in colored lights. Get a fruitcake as a gift and regift it to someone else. And when I became a teenager, I wanted to get kissed under the mistletoe.

Yes, I liked our small and delicate menorah with its blue and white candles that we lit for eight nights. It was fun to spin dreidels and eat chocolate Hanukkah gelt. But those activities were overshadowed by the glitter, sparkle and songs of Christmas. I just wanted a piece of that.

Now as an adult, I see the beauty and mystery of my own faith. I cherish my heritage and the way we celebrate. I've learned that enjoying the rituals of someone else's holiday can be a source of fun instead of a source of longing. And, yes, I can be found driving through neighborhoods looking at Christmas lights—and eating my share of gingerbread cookies—each and every December.

Strangers on a Campus

After addressing the auditorium filled with parents of prospective students, the President of the College said, "It's your turn now to ask us questions that you have about our college."

A man in a beige-and-green striped polo asked, "Does campus security carry any handguns?"

I thought that was an odd question.

"No," the Director of Campus Security said. "They can't because they're not commissioned officers."

"Well, then," the same man asked, "is there a lockdown procedure in place?"

"All college campuses have that," the Director said.

The man looked like he was processing another question, but before he could articulate it, a woman in front of me raised her hand. "I have a few questions about students who have internships in New York. When they're in New York, do you have anyone from the college with them?"

"No, we do not. We have no control over what happens in New York."

The audience went silent.

Then the woman turned and asked the Director of the Health Center, "Do you have psychological services for the students?"

"Yes, we do," she said. "We look out for our students. That isn't to say that we watch them 24/7, it's just that this school is small enough that if a student missed a couple of classes we would hear about it."

I found myself almost shaking my head in disbelief. Why are these parents so worried about security and mental health? What about academics, social life, athletics and job placement? I had heard parents ask a question here and there about safety when I had been on other college visits with my daughter Olivia, but they weren't the first questions to be asked.

Then I realized that we were only an hour's train ride away from New York City, not far from what was once the World Trade Center. I remembered what my daughter told me about her friend's mother, who teaches at a high school in New Jersey: twenty of her students lost a parent to 9/11. Nearly everyone who lived within an hour of New York City either suffered horrific loss or was close to someone who did. I can't even imagine how that would feel, even now, years later. This was the audience I was sitting with—a post-9/11, anxious, fearful group.

My phone vibrated—a text from my daughter. "I don't want to go to college here."

"Wow," I thought. She must not be having a good time on the college tour. In the past year and a half, we'd been to at least ten colleges, and I'd never gotten a text like that before.

"Let's meet at the car," I texted back.

The first thing Olivia said when she got in the front seat

was, "The students I talked to didn't seem to know that much about the school."

"I noticed that too," I said. "The girl who took us on the parent tour told me when we walked up to the auditorium that she had never been in the building. I thought, that's not a good sign. I mean aren't there any performances or events that go on in there?"

"A couple of the students talked about ghosts," Olivia said, "how the school has ghosts that roam a couple of buildings and scare the students."

"Somehow that wouldn't be a selling point for me," I said. Olivia and I laughed.

"It's funny, but I've had a bit of a creepy feeling ever since we arrived on this campus," I said. "Maybe it's the ghosts." We paused and looked at the gothic architecture surrounding us. It was a sunny day, but I could picture the buildings in a dark storm, spooky and untamed.

I've heard parents say that their children could step foot on a campus and say right then whether they'd like to go to that college or not. I used to think that was ridiculous, but now I get it.

That definitely happened here. It was a relief to drive away, leaving the ghosts behind us.

Pitter Patter All Night Long

What I remember most was hearing footsteps that came and went past my tiny room all night long. Then I'd hear a door—the bathroom door at the end of the hall—open and close. A brief, momentary silence would ensue and then just as I was about to drift off, the footsteps would start up again. Sometimes the bathroom visitor was also a cougher. Sometimes there was so much hacking that it was a bit scary, like the cougher was choking to death.

I was hoping it was smoker's cough and not something contagious. How people could pee all night long and cough endlessly made no sense to me. I was nineteen years old and wondering, Who are these students? I hadn't met any students who behaved like this during my time in Europe.

I had arrived in London alone around midnight. My study abroad program had ended. I'd been doing some traveling with friends and I needed a place to spend the night before going back to the States the next day. I'd thought this place was a student hostel, but I was beginning to wonder.

My thin beige blanket was not keeping me warm. A few times, when I heard loud footsteps pacing just outside my room, I looked at the flimsy lock on the door and worried someone would break in. And I was hoping I wouldn't have to use the bathroom because I didn't want to run into those strange, hacking people in the night. Then I realized I'd have to see them in the morning. I thought of leaving but knew I was far better off here than wandering the streets of London at 3:00 a.m.

Morning came. The sun shone through my torn sheer curtains. It was finally quiet. What time was it? I threw on some clothes and opened the door. No one was in the hall. I took the staircase down and almost gasped. There were several old men sitting in the lobby. They looked up at me, surprised. One smiled a toothless friendly smile. The men held paper coffee cups and puffed away at their cigarettes.

"Good morning," I said, trying to sound chipper.

"Morning," a few said to me in unison.

So much for cheap housing, I thought. This wasn't a student hostel—this was a flophouse. Oh my God, I thought to myself, I stayed in a flophouse.

I went right up to the lady at the counter to check out. Her skin was so pale and her hair such a faded gray that I wondered if she had ever seen the sun. She looked surprised to see me. I'm sure I didn't look a thing like their regular customers. I handed her my money. "Cheerio," she said.

"Cheerio," I said as the door slammed behind me.

A World of Its Own

My son, Sam, has a saltwater aquarium, and we heard through his grapevine of reef enthusiasts that there was a marine store about forty-five minutes away that carried some beautiful corals. So we decided to go on an adventure to this small Ohio town that we'd never been to.

There was no Google image of this store, so we had to imagine it. It's interesting how your mind creates a visual of something when it really has no idea what it might really look like. We both pictured an old building, in an old downtown. Boy, were we wrong.

Instead we found ourselves driving down a winding country road. My GPS suddenly said that we had arrived at our destination and I caught a glimpse, at thirty miles per hour, of a wooden sign with the word "Marine" on it.

I quickly turned in. To my right was a seventies, rust-colored brick ranch house with an old farmhouse behind it. A wooden building stood a short distance away.

As I was parking, I noticed that the side door of the house was wide open. I could see the family room furniture. How weird, I thought. And then, two big dogs rushed up to the car, a friendly-looking Golden with a red bandana and a large mutt with a face like a Great Dane that I was a little wary of.

"Come on, Mom," Sam said. "They're nice dogs."

His words put me at ease. He knows me too well, I thought. We stepped out of the car and the dogs nuzzled us repeatedly, barely letting us out of the parking area. Next we had to figure out where the marine store was. I had a creepy feeling that we could be misinterpreted as trespassers. I didn't want to open strange doors—I didn't want us to get shot. (On the way here we'd passed several gun stores.) I took out my phone and called the number for the marine store, but no one answered, adding to my concern.

"Mom, it's over there." Sam pointed to a sign leading to the building in the distance.

"Are you sure?"

"Yeah, I'm sure," he said, looking at me like I was worrying too much, which it turned out I was.

We walked to the building and opened the door. Inside we saw tanks filled with fish. A big puffer in a lone tank stared at us like we were lost. "Hello, hello," I called. There was silence and I continued to feel uncomfortable. Was there anyone here?

As we turned down an aisle and walked toward the back, we saw two men in the distance looking at corals. They must not have heard us over the hum of the tank pumps.

"Hi," one of the men said. "I'm Jack. Can I help you?"

"Yes," I said. "We're here to look at some corals."

"Well, you've come to the right place," he said. "I'm helping this gentleman. I'll be with you in a few minutes."

While waiting, we gazed at the mysterious, magnificent

corals. It seemed so unlikely that they flourished here on this Ohio farm far from their ocean beds. They seemed well taken care of, and on closer inspection, their delicate beauty reminded me of my parents' floral glass paperweights that had entranced me as a child. I felt that same trance-like sensation as I watched the water gently lapping across each coral.

"Look, Mom, look at those Zoanthids," Sam said excitedly, pointing them out to me. I saw what appeared to be miniscule orange, green and red buds.

"They kind of look like flower buds," I said.

"Those are polyps, Mom."

I inspected them more closely. Each one is a world of its own, I thought. I was happy we'd made the trip.

Looking at the water and the corals and the occasional fish swimming through the flat-bed tanks was peaceful, even though the getting here had been a little dicey. As Sam bargained with Jack over a couple of corals he wanted, I thought, It's funny, the next time we come back, we will not feel like strangers.

Strangers Using Strange Words

As I get older, some words become stranger and stranger. Words that mean one thing to me mean something else to Generation Y—Gen Y for short.

Call me old-fashioned. I know words can change meaning over time, but for goodness sakes, "shut up" just means "shut up." It means "shut your mouth and don't utter another word or I'll be even more pissed off than I already am."

I've been told "shut up" at least three times lately by different Gen Y women. What they mean to say is, "Like, wow, what you're saying is really wild, cool or unreal!" All I hear is something ugly.

What worries me is, what's happened to boundaries? Don't they know that I'm not in their inner circle where their slang belongs?

That brings me to another phrase that I find offensive: "hook up."

I don't want my friends to say, "Let's hook up around 7 for dinner," and, yes, that has happened. Just ask me if I'd like to get together and have dinner.

"You are your words" is what I want to say to people who don't use language responsibly or respectfully. We're gifted with the good fortune of having the freedom to use words as we wish in America—we should take pride in our words and use them thoughtfully. Without thinking about what our words really mean, we can lose our civility.

Medicine for What Ails You

"Thank you for the pot stickers," I said to the elderly Chinese woman at the counter. "They smell delicious."

"My English not so good," she answered. She smiled at me and I didn't know if she understood what I had said. How difficult life must be in America if you don't speak English, or for that matter in any country where you don't speak the national language. Her smile was her way of dealing with her difficult situation and I admired her for it.

How ironic, I thought, that this morning on my way to the grocery store I had seen a lone bumper sticker on the red Hatchback in front of me that read "Welcome to America. Please speak English." I saw in the rear view mirror that the driver was a middle-aged man with a receding hairline. How dumb, I thought. Not only is that an insensitive thing to say, but if you don't speak English, you're not going to be able to read the bumper sticker anyway, so what's the point?

The Chinese woman handed me the bill and I saw that her arm looked like it had burns on it, or welts. She seemed happy that I noticed. "Mosquito. Mosquito," she repeated.

She knew the word "mosquito" and the bites looked bad. I recognized what was wrong because my family is very allergic to mosquitoes. "You need Benadryl," I said to her. She tried to say the word. "Bendra, Bendra."

She handed me a tiny notepad and pencil. I wrote down the name of the medicine, wondering if that would help her. At that moment I felt a helpless barrier between us and

I hoped that someone would translate to her what I had written.

"Daughter coming," she said, and I understood this to be a daughter who spoke English.

She reached underneath a counter and showed me a small amber-colored bottle covered in Chinese letters. "Oil," she said to me. Maybe it was some sort of topical pain relief, but if it was, it was not helping her.

I was fascinated by the words on the small bottle and she let me hold it in my hand. I turned it around and wondered what kind of ailments the oil treated. I've always been intrigued by Eastern medicine. This was the first time I was privy to seeing a bottle of medicine from China.

"You might need to see a doctor," I said to her, looking at her arm once again.

"Doctor," she repeated and smiled at me.

"I hope you feel better," I said.

Even though we did not speak the same language, I knew that we had connected anyway. She needed to tell somebody about her mosquito bites and I was there to listen and advise. She was not able to speak English very well but she was contributing to society by working, which stimulated the economy. And her pot stickers are delicious.

I wish I could find the owner of that nasty bumper sticker and tell him to remove it. There are so many more problems to worry about in this world. How about having a more positive bumper sticker like "Save the Planet" or "Make Peace Not War"?

Maybe he needs a taste of his own medicine—we could drop him in a foreign country where no English is spoken and see how well he fares.

LIKE-MINDED STRANGERS

The Artist in the Paint Department

"Can you match this old paint?" I asked the bearded young man at the hardware store.

"Well, let's take a look," he said. He carefully opened the can with a flathead screwdriver.

"Cool old paint," he said, as he stared into the can. "Do you know that old paint cans are collectible?"

"You're kidding," I said.

"Look on eBay."

I took out my phone and checked. Sure enough, there were some vintage paint cans. "Wow," I said. "Who knew that Ford Taffy Tan Synthetic Enamel vintage paint has a starting bid of $5.50 with 6 bids on it!"

He smiled at me.

"I love eBay," I told him. "I learn so much looking at vintage objects."

"What have you been looking at lately?"

"Well…" I paused. He's so much younger than me, will he know what I'm talking about? What the heck, I decided. "I was looking at some apothecary bottles," I said.

A big grin appeared on his face and his friendly hazel eyes became even friendlier. I knew that we had connected over something, but I didn't know what.

"I make turned wood apothecary bottles," he said. "I'm Appalachian, and I guess it's just in my DNA. I'm self-taught."

What are the odds, I wondered, that I'd ended up looking at apothecary bottles in the first place? Pretty unlikely, I'd say. I'd been looking at one thing on eBay that led me to another thing that led to another thing. And what's the chance that today, in the paint department of a hardware store, I would meet a craftsman of turned wood apothecary bottles?

"I'll show you some pictures of my bottles," he said and he took out his phone.

"They're beautiful," I said. "You must be very proud of your work."

"I enjoy it. Here, I'll match this paint for you."

I could hear the faint sounds of paint mixing, sloshing back and forth in cans on a machine. That's a comforting sound, I thought. Colors are being created. It's cool that he knows how to mix them.

As I waited, a small line of people formed behind me.

"Here you go," he said, as he put the quart down.

"Thanks, and good luck with your bottles," I said.

He smiled and then asked the man behind me, "Sir, what can I help you with?"

Southern Sisterhood

I'm a Northerner who loves Southern expressions. Maybe because I'm a writer, I soak them up and marvel at them. Play them over and over in my mind. Sometimes, I write about them.

Like yesterday at breakfast at my hotel in Nashville. I wasn't getting the best service. My coffee cup sat empty. The waitress was overworked. She was covering the floor, as they say. So when I finally got her to pour me one, I said, "Can I keep the carafe?"

She said, "Yes, ma'am," and a woman a couple of tables over said, "I'm with you, sister, on that."

With a friendly Southern turn of phrase she had fashioned us into sisters, connected through our mutual need to savor our steaming beverage to remind ourselves that the day has begun.

She was a middle-aged woman like me, elegant in that Southern way, all put together before breakfast. I admired that. A stranger to me a minute ago, but now a Southern sister. We sipped our coffees. She gave me a friendly nod and I nodded back.

A Sweet Connection

I'm deciding between the large cotton balls and the jumbo-size ones when I hear a woman an aisle or so over say, "Where are the turtles? They used to be here, but now they're not." She sounds a bit flustered, like she can't believe that they've been moved under her watch.

Then I hear another woman say, "That's what I'm looking for too."

"Jeanette, Jeanette, where are those DeMet's TURTLES?" I hear the first woman ask.

A minute later I see the cashier leading the two candy seekers down the center aisle of the store. How many times does this woman come here to buy turtles anyway?

"They're over here in the fancy candy department," Jeanette says, pointing at the pretty display. "Fancy candy," she mumbles, shaking her head and walking back to the register.

I decide to follow the two women, wanting to know what I've been missing. I love turtles, but I have never thought of pharmacies as the center of all things turtle.

The women shriek with joy as they find the hidden turtles. I'm surprised to see that CVS has distinguished between the haves and the have-nots of the chocolate world. The trendy Ghirardelli and Lindor brands are displayed proudly at eye level. The DeMet's have been relegated to the bottom shelf. But they are on sale: two 7-ounce bags for $7.

"So these are the famous turtles?" I say to the women.

"Yes, yes," they say and they each grab two bags. Then I reach for one. I have to see if they are really better than the average turtle.

A tall, angular woman appears from the shampoo aisle. "I overheard you all, and where are those turtles? I've got to try them." She says it like she has been missing the party and doesn't want to be left out. I like her immediately.

When we're all in the checkout line together, I'm practically laughing aloud at how one woman's turtle quest is influencing the buying habits of what appear to be the only three other shoppers in the store. Jeanette, however, does not seem impressed.

Back in my car, I rip open one of the miniature, individually wrapped turtles and eat one, then another.

Curious person that I am, I decide to check on the history of DeMet's TURTLES, and Google the company on my phone. After all, there aren't any famous confections named after lions, tigers or bears. I find out that TURTLE is a trademark of Johnson's Candy Company, which became DeMet's Candy Company in 1923. Turns out that these candies got their name in 1918, when a "dipper" commented to a salesman that they looked a lot like, yes, turtles. All these years I didn't know that I wasn't really eating TURTLES, only imitations.

I unwrap one last TURTLE. They are small, so I don't feel too guilty. The heat from the sun envelops me and the pecans, caramel and chocolate melt in my mouth. Soooo good, I think.

And then I wonder, are they really that good, or is it the influence of two TURTLE-impassioned strangers?

Revisiting the Roselawn Post Office

Yes, it's another stranger encounter from the Roselawn Post Office. Same place, different day, different year, different story.

I walk through drifts of snow and a slushy pool of water to the entrance of the post office, and take my place in line behind a man just out of the cusp of teenhood. As the two of us, bored and fidgety, stare at the glass case of stamps between us and the counter, a sudden click clack of heels pulses past us. It is the sound of shoes on a mission.

The black stilettos belong to a woman in her late twenties with ringlets of long auburn hair and a too-short black skirt. I immediately decide I don't trust her. Come on, who wears stilettos in the snow?

She brushes past us and approaches the counter without acknowledging us, holding at least five letters. That's it, I say to myself and blurt out, "There's a line here."

"Oh," she stammers. "I didn't mean to cut you off—I just need to mail these."

"Well, you never know," I say.

A postal clerk takes her letters and the stiletto-heeled woman leaves in a hurry, averting her eyes from us.

The almost-man teen turns to me and says, "I like your style."

"Thank you," I say and add, almost confessionally. "Well,

if she had been a big mean man, I don't think I would have said anything."

He pauses, then says, "I've got your back."

This man I had just met "had my back." Now it's not every day that a stranger takes on having your back. This was a moment to bear witness to. I like his style too, I thought. Suddenly, I imagined us in a Postal Fairy Tale, where the big mean man comes into the post office, tries to pull a fast one on the two of us and we go postal—me calling out the bad guy, the young man punching him out while the rest of the people in the post office cheer and clap in support of our teen hero.

Before the big mean man wakes up, the two of us escape through the back door of the post office and jump onto an awaiting wooden sled with bright red runners. We vanish down the hill at supersonic speed and land with a thud in a large pile of snow that looks good enough to eat, like Reddi-wip. (Of course we land safely; this is a fairy tale.) We struggle to get up because we're laughing so hard, astonished at our fantastical escape.

"See, I've got your back," he says, grinning, and gives me a quick hug goodbye.

"I've got yours, too," I say, hugging him back.

In the next scene he's home and his mother is asking, "How'd you get so wet?"

"Oh, Mom," he says, "It's a long story, but basically, I wiped out in the snow on my way back from the post office."

Delivery Shot

One day several months ago, a thin middle-aged UPS man with salt-and-pepper hair came to drop off a package at our house. My son Sam was shooting hoops in the driveway. The man put our package down and lifted his hands in a universal gesture that means "pass me the ball." That wordless moment initiated a common bond—a man, a boy, and a basketball.

This went on for a while without my knowing about it— until one day at dinner when Sam told me that if he is out playing hoops and sees that UPS man coming, he's at the ready to toss the ball his way. And the UPS man is at the ready to catch it.

"How long do you two play for?" I asked, knowing how tight a schedule those UPS drivers operate on.

"About five times, until he makes a bank shot."

"What's his name?"

"I don't know."

The UPS man doesn't know Sam's name either. And I realize neither of them need to. What they share is a moment of hoops, a small break in their day when they don't have to think about anything else but the ball swishing through the net.

Tea with Strangers

I read a great article in *Forbes* by Jon Youshaei called "How to Meet Amazing People Without Sleazy Networking: Insights from 6,220 Conversations." He wrote about Ankit Shah, the founder of "Tea with Strangers," who connects people who have never met over cups of tea so they can share stories with each other. As Ankit says on his website, "Everyone around you is a person, loaded with stories that you can't even begin to fathom. They're different from yours, but the fact that we all have them is what brings us together."

Ankit has a community of hosts in different cities who organize sessions of tea and conversation for small groups of strangers. There's no agenda and there are no strings attached—genuine communication between strangers is the only goal. His reason is to "make our cities feel more like neighborhoods" because he believes that "we're more connected than ever before, but we're more alone." Real face-to-face conversations create a sense of belonging and community that makes life better for all of us.

I couldn't agree with him more. Why not meet someone new every chance you get? There's always an opportunity for a fresh perspective—it only takes a few minutes to reach out to a stranger.

I wish Ankit and his "Tea with Strangers" project all the best. Just think, he's creating community one cup of tea at a time.

Rush-Hour Rainbow

We often feel like we're all alone when we're driving by ourselves down a highway, insulated in our own vehicles. But we're not. Not really.

Like the other morning when I was heading south on 71, and all the traffic slowed. Was it an accident, a stalled car or construction that was affecting our joint rush hour?

It was not. This time, what had caused all the braking was a multicolored rainbow that arched from the left, fading a bit as it made its way across the sky.

It was a magical moment, but here I was on the highway. There was no time to stop and gaze at it. However, like my fellow drivers, I could slow down.

I couldn't remember ever having seen such a large rainbow. I searched my memory but came up empty, except for the vision of Judy Garland singing "Somewhere Over the Rainbow." So I sang it myself. And then I wondered how many other people in this long parade of slowed automobiles might be singing "Somewhere Over the Rainbow" too.

There was no way to know, of course. But as I watched the last seconds of our rainbow before it disappeared from view, I smiled at this reminder that we're connected with a myriad of strangers in a myriad of ways, including this brilliant spectrum of colors that we briefly got to share.

RESOURCES

Research by behavioral scientists suggests that we are happier when we talk to strangers. If you want to find out more about the benefits of connecting with strangers and learn fun, easy ways to interact with them, here is a collection of ideas, tips, information and stories.

You can also find these links and the posts I wrote that go into more detail about them on my blog, **strangersihaveknown.com**.

REAP HEALTH BENEFITS.
Nicole Frehsée speaks about the health perks of sharing positive emotion with strangers in her article in *O, The Oprah Magazine*, "The Love Connection": **http://www.nicolefrehsee.com/wp-content/ uploads/2013/01/Love-QA.pdf**

LEARN HOW TO TALK WITH ANYONE.
Malavika Varadan shares "7 Ways to Make a Conversation with Anyone" in her TED talk from Mumbai: **https://www.youtube.com/watch?v=F4Zu5ZZAG7I**

STRIKE UP A CONVERSATION ON YOUR DAILY COMMUTE.
Justine Hofherr's article, "Research on how to make your commute more productive and less depressing," on Boston.com will encourage you to talk with the person you're sitting next to, and also offers two other suggestions: http://www.boston.com/jobs/jobs-news/2016/03/16/3-better-ways-to-spend-your-work-commute

TRUST YOUR INSTINCTS ABOUT WHICH STRANGERS TO TALK TO.

An article by Yasmin Anwar on UC Berkeley's Greater Good Science Center's [GGSC] website shares research about what's genetically behind first impressions in "Is That Stranger Trustworthy? You'll Know in 20 Seconds":
http://greatergood.berkeley.edu/article/item/ is_that_stranger_trustworthy_youll_know_in_20_ seconds

MAKE YOUR OWN LUCK

Did you know that luck is actually a learnable skill? One of the missions of UC Berkeley's Greater Good Science Center is to give parents tips for making happy kids and being happy themselves. In this GGSC video, Christine Carter, Ph.D. and Lindsay Reed Maimes discuss "how we can teach our kids to make their own luck" here. You'll learn some tips for yourself, too:
https://www.youtube.com/watch?v=QHfkIf5tXqY &feature=youtu.be

SPARK CONVERSATION AND CONNECTION.

You may never come across a "Meet-up in the Ball Pit" like these encounters filmed by SoulPancake on Oprah's Super Soul Sunday, but the conversation starters are great:
https://www.youtube.com/watch?v=qKrSG64J_Bo

FIND INSPIRATION THROUGH "HUMANS OF NEW YORK."

Join the over 17 million folks on Facebook who follow Brandon Stanton's photos and interviews of New Yorkers eager to share their stories:

https://www.facebook.com/humansofnewyork
http://www.humansofnewyork.com

HAVE TEA WITH A STRANGER.

Founder Ankit Shah brings people in a number
of different cities together through his "Tea with
Strangers" website. You can request to have tea with
a group of people you don't know yet, and even
host a "Tea with Strangers" yourself:
http://www.teawithstrangers.com/

LEARN "HOW TO MEET AMAZING PEOPLE WITHOUT SLEAZY NETWORKING."

Get to
know more about Brandon Stanton and Ankit
Shah, as well as tips and insights about connecting
with strangers, through Jon Youshaei's article
"How to Meet Amazing People Without Sleazy
Networking: Insights from 6,220 Conversations"
in *Forbes* magazine:
http://www.forbes.com/sites/
jonyoushaei/2015/05/13/how-to-meet-amazing-
people-without-sleazy-networking-insights-from-
6220-conversations/#1074d5363823

SAVOR STORIES AND IMAGES OF STRANGERS WHO'D LIKE TO SEE EACH OTHER AGAIN.

Missed Connections, a book by Sophie Blackall,
pairs her own creative drawings with her favorite
"'Missed Connections', the online listings posted by
lovelorn strangers hoping to reconnect":
http://www.sophieblackall.com/missed-
connections-2

WRITE A LOVE LETTER TO A STRANGER.

Hannah Brencher, founder of a global organization called "The World Needs More Love Letters," believes passionately in the power of loving words on a page. Listen to her tell her moving story through her TED talk, and then hop over to her website to learn how to write your own love letters to strangers: **https://www.ted.com/talks/hannah_brencher_love_ letters_to_strangers?language=en http://www.moreloveletters.com**

ACKNOWLEDGMENTS

There are two people that I want to thank first and foremost. Without them this book would not have happened.

To Maureen Ryan Griffin, talented writer, teacher, editor, mentor and friend, who has helped me make my writing dreams come true.

To my wonderful and loving daughter Olivia. Thank you for your creative insights and for helping me with the technical aspects of blogging and all things social media. You were there to assist week after week, always with a smile on your face and an open heart.

I know that it takes a village to raise a child, but I believe it also takes a village to raise a writer.

And with that, much love to my husband Steve, the eternal optimist who always rooted for me to get my stories turned into a book. "Just say no to naysayers" is one of your mottos, and one that I live by because of you.

To my marvelous son Sam. Thanks for taking the time, even though you're a busy teenager, to pat your mom on the back and ask her how her writing is going. Also, thanks for listening to my impromptu stranger stories at the dinner table. There were probably times you weren't entertained, but you kept that to yourself.

Heartfelt love and gratitude to my parents, Nancy and Philip Kotler. You filled my life with books, strong values and the love of people from the very start. Mom, you were a role model by being a college English professor. Dad, you know you were my first author role model. Watching you night after night throughout my childhood as you created your numerous books and subsequent editions on your typewriter, then your word processor, and then your computer, was magical to me and a big inspiration for my writing.

To my sisters Amy Heifitz and Jessica Stahl: you're the best cheerleaders anyone could have.

A big shout-out to Women Writing for a Change in Cincinnati, Ohio. Thanks for ten years of writing circles, friendship, laughter and stories.

To Sydney Lieberman (1944 – 2015), my favorite high school teacher, who was warm, witty, super bright, everything a teacher should be. How appropriate that he won a Golden Apple award for teaching in 1986.

Syd, (yes, we were allowed to call him by his first name), thanks for believing in me and my writing. You taught me so much about language, life and the importance of family. It didn't surprise me to hear that in your second career you became a storyteller. Not just any storyteller, but the first one hired by NASA, who then went on to win the 2013 National Storytelling Network's lifetime achievement award.

A blog needs readers, and I'm grateful for mine. A special thanks to my loyal blog followers who took the time to share comments and insights on my posts, especially Hope Felton-Miller, Marion Brown, Kathy Wade, Billy Jacobson, Vi Bronner, Angela Retzios and Ann Kaplan.

And, finally, many thanks to all the strangers I've met, especially those whose stories appear here, to all the strangers I've yet to meet and to all people who take the time to no longer be strangers to one another.

MELISSA KOTLER SCHWARTZ

ABOUT THE AUTHOR

Melissa Kotler Schwartz is a writer, teacher and human interest aficionado. She volunteers as a children's literacy tutor and teaches autobiography at Osher Lifelong Learning Institute (OLLI) at the University of Cincinnati.

Since she wishes there was more justice in the world, she loves reading mysteries and solving them. She is a member of Mystery Writers of America and Sisters in Crime and is at work on a mystery novel.

Her most recent mystery involved an odd animal odor she encountered upon opening a basement window. "Squirrel," she announced to no one. Case solved. She is confident she could become a professional wine sniffer if she decided to switch careers and often thinks about insuring her nose.

She lives with her family in Cincinnati, Ohio, and her favorite pastimes include playing with dogs (especially her own), knitting scarves she'll never wear and researching ad nauseam anything she doesn't know about but thinks she ought to.

You can connect with her at strangersihaveknown.com.

Made in the USA
Lexington, KY
03 January 2017